Everyone Wins!

A Citizen's Guide to Development

Everyone Wins!

A Citizen's Guide to Development

Richard D. Klein

PLANNERS PRESS

AMERICAN PLANNING ASSOCIATION

Chicago, Illinois
Washington, D.C.

Copyright 1990 by the American Planning Association
1313 E. 60th St., Chicago, IL 60637
Paperback edition ISBN 0-918286-63-8
Hardbound edition ISBN 0-918286-64-6
Library of Congress Catalog Number 89-82154

To

Jim Gracie, an environmental genius
and my mentor

Malcolm King, the greatest conservationist
I have had the pleasure to know

Barbara Taylor, my adviser,
inspiration, and dearest friend

Contents

1

Getting Started

WHO SHOULD READ THIS BOOK?

In writing this book, I had one purpose in mind: to help you to protect your home, your community, and the environment from the damages associated with land development. The book is intended to serve as a guide for those having little experience with development issues. But the winning strategies offered in the following pages will also help the veteran community activist to be even more effective in dealing with development.

WHAT IS DEVELOPMENT?

For the purpose of this book, development is defined as the conversion of rural land to residential and commercial uses, such as shopping centers, schools, business parks, and highways. But I have also used the strategies described here to deal with activities encompassed by a broader definition of land development, such as mining, landfills, logging operations, solid waste incinerators, and many other land-use alterations that may affect adjacent residents, a community, or the environment.

WHAT THIS BOOK WILL DO FOR YOU?

This book is designed to help you find the easiest and least expensive solution for your development-related problems. In the following pages, I will show you:

- How to preserve land in an undeveloped condition through: acquisition by a government agency, a land trust; a foundation, or other

1

preservations entities; an easement program; or a variety of other mechanisms.

- How to determine if local regulations will allow the site to be developed.
- How to learn if real estate market conditions favor development of the tract.
- How to determine if the site can be developed in a way that will threaten your interests.
- How to use the law to ensure that your interests are fully protected.
- How to launch a political-action campaign to encourage decision makers to support your cause.
- How to raise the funds needed to hire experts and lawyers and to cover the many other costs associated with your campaign.
- How to mobilize volunteers for political-action tactics, such as letter writing, packing a hearing, or jamming the phone lines into city hall.
- How to combine all these steps into an effective campaign strategy.
- How to protect your gains from losses due to broken promises or faulty enforcement programs.

STRATEGIES FOR DEALING WITH DEVELOPMENT

This book will help you to examine three strategies for satisfying your development-related needs:

- Land preservation (either partial or total);
- Delaying development;
- Seeking solutions that can be implemented without prohibiting development.

A tract of land may be preserved in an undeveloped state either through acquisition, a conservation easement, a transfer of development rights, or a limited development venture. Any of these options can be used to preserve either all of the tract or only a part of it.

Development can be delayed through legal action designed to forestall the issuance of permits and other approvals necessary to begin development. Delays can also be achieved by using public pressure to force government to withhold permits and approvals, or to apply a very stringent interpretation of development regulations to the project in question.

If you are concerned about one minor aspect of a proposed development venture, it may make more sense to resolve that particular concern than to launch an expensive, time-consuming campaign to preserve the tract or to delay development.

What are the pros and cons of these three strategies?

Land preservation is generally a strategy with limited applicability. Acquisition funds are reserved for tracts that have some unique attribute, such as exceptional natural beauty, or for properties valued by a large number of taxpayers. Opportunities to preserve land through the use of easements, a transfer of development rights, or a limited development venture are infrequent. But these are nothing more than generalizations. The property of concern to you may well be the exception.

It may cost $5,000 to $40,000 in legal fees to delay the development of a site. Delay can be an effective strategy for buying time, but the time will be worth the expense only if you can delay the venture long enough for some change to occur that may bring you closer to your ultimate goal. Delay can also be an effective means of convincing an uncooperative property owner to negotiate in good faith. This assumes, of course, that you are interested in negotiation. If your sole objective is to kill the project, negotiation is pointless. While it is frequently possible to delay development, killing a project permanently is seldom realistic. If you defeat a development proposal today, you may find yourself fighting the same battle over a new proposal five years from now.

Of these three strategies, the third—seeking solutions to specific concerns—is usually the easiest and least expensive. Land preservation is ultimately the most costly, but may involve less heartburn and time than a delaying action. Killing a project tends to produce the least permanent solution. Once a preservation option is implemented or a solution for a specific concern is carried out, the effect of the property upon your interests remains fixed. Going for a permanent delay can be like battling the mythical beast that never quite dies, but rises again and again to threaten you till the end of time.

SECRETS OF SUCCESS

Over the past 20 years, I have helped hundreds of groups to win development issues. Consistently, the groups that won employed the following secrets of success.

Strive for a Win-Win Solution

Is it necessary to stop a development project to protect your interests? If not, look for a solution that satisfies you and imposes the fewest restrictions on how the property owner can use his land. While any development project can be stopped, it is rarely easy to do so. It takes lots of time and money. It is far easier to convince the property owner to modify, rather than abandon, his development plans. So seek a win-win solution before launching a campaign to halt a development venture.

Don't Delay; Start Today!

Time is frequently the greatest enemy in dealing with development. It is easier to:

- Preserve land in a natural state before the property owner becomes committed to development;
- Modify a development proposal while the plans are still being drawn up;
- Stop a development before bulldozers arrive at the site;
- Raise the money and recruit the volunteers needed to deal with development when a deadline is months away as opposed to a few weeks.

So begin early.

Assume the Positive

When dealing with a development issue, it is seldom possible to operate solely on the basis of facts. Invariably, one must make a number of assumptions. I urge you to think positively and avoid negative assumptions.

- Assume that others want to support your efforts with dollars and volunteer hours; don't assume that you must bear all costs and responsibilities alone.
- Assume that elected officials, the property owner, and other decision makers will be receptive to your concerns; don't assume that no one will care how a development proposal may affect you.
- Assume that solutions can be found that will satisfy both you and the property owner; don't assume that halting development is the only answer.

Pursue a Combined Political and Legal Strategy

The objective of political action is to convince decision makers— mostly elected officials—to support your cause. Legal action serves to ensure that a proposed development venture complies with all applicable laws. Groups that pursue a good legal strategy win about half the time. Groups following a sound political strategy, combined with a good legal strategy, win more than 90 percent of the time!

Hustle!

Clearly define your goals. Investigate all the options that may lead to the attainment of your goals. Decide which options have the greatest potential for success; then, starting with the most promising, pursue each option until you run out of time and money. Each additional option you pursue creates another factor working in your favor. The key to success is to get as many of the most promising options working for you as quickly as possible.

CHAPTER

2

What Would
Victory Look Like?

What do you hope to accomplish? What damages do you wish to prevent? Do you benefit in some way from an undeveloped piece of land? Will these benefits be lost if the land is developed? Is it necessary to halt development of a tract of land in order to protect your interests? Could the tract be developed in a way that allows both you and the property owner to achieve your goals? The answers to these questions can serve as a definition of "what victory would look like."

Why bother with these questions when, after all, the whole issue can be resolved simply by blocking all attempts to develop a piece of land? The answer is equally simple: stopping a development project can be expensive and terribly time consuming.

Before launching a campaign to halt a development venture, look for opportunities to reach a compromise with the property owner. The ideal compromise protects your interests and imposes the fewest restrictions on how the property owner may use his land. For example, if you are concerned that development may increase the student population beyond the capacity of local schools, two solutions might be available: prohibit development or increase school capacity. The first solution obviously imposes severe restrictions on property owners wishing to develop their land, while the second may satisfy both you and the owner.

To work towards this ideal, you must clearly identify the damages you hope to prevent and the benefits you would like to retain. Collectively, the damages and benefits can be formed into statements concerning the goals of your campaign.

Once you have identified your goals, it will be easier to determine if a solution exists that may be mutually agreeable to you and the property owner.

WHAT DAMAGES DO YOU WISH TO PREVENT?

I assume that you already have a few damages in mind. But perhaps there are other impacts you have not considered. Think about all the different ways a piece of land might be developed. Find out what uses are permitted on the site by local zoning regulations or other laws. Consider the various phases of the land development process: clearing of vegetation, burning of debris (if permitted), grading and filling, and the modification of waterways and other features. How would each phase affect your interests? Finally, take a look at others who may be affected by development of the tract. What damages might they list if asked to consider the preceding questions?

A number of factors are presented in Chapter 5, each of which may be affected by development. I urge you to review the topic headings in Chapter 5 as an aid in compiling a complete list of damages.

WHAT BENEFITS WOULD YOU LIKE TO RETAIN?

Think about the property as it currently exists. What beneficial uses are made of the property? What safeguards does the property provide? How would these benefits and safeguards change if the property were developed? How would these changes affect your interests? How would other people answer these questions? Following are several examples of benefits that may be associated with an undeveloped tract of land:

- Provides a buffer from noise and other nuisances;
- Offers a place to hike, walk, picnic, watch birds, and pursue other outdoor activities;
- Supports essential agricultural activities;
- Provides a unique habitat for rare or endangered wildlife or plants;
- The present character of site safeguards historic or archeological features.

WHAT BENEFITS WOULD RESULT
FROM DEVELOPMENT?

Are there any problems associated with the property that might be solved through development? Will development provide services or opportunities vital to the welfare of the community? Perhaps several of the following benefits may apply to your situation. Development may:
- Attract companies offering more or better jobs;
- Expand the tax base;
- Eliminate nuisances, such as dangerous pits, crime-prone areas, dilapidated buildings, etc;
- Enhance adjacent property values;
- Create opportunities to replace aging sewer lines, improve streets, build new schools;
- Improve environmental quality by eliminating a source of air, water, land, or noise pollution.

WHAT ARE YOUR GOALS?

Consider each of the damages that may result from development, the benefits of keeping the tract in its present state, and any benefits that may result from development. Combine all three into clear statements concerning the goals of your effort.

The next chapter will explain how to find an easy way of reaching your goals. The ideal solution should:
- Eliminate the damages;
- Maintain the benefits presently derived from the land;
- Allow sufficient development to occur so the benefits associated with a change in land use will come about;
- Allow the property owner to attain his goals.

3

Try the Easy
Solutions First

A full-scale campaign to deal with a development issue can be quite expensive and may require hundreds of hours of your time. Before launching such an ambitious effort, take a look at your options for reaching your goals quickly and painlessly.

If a quick, easy victory is possible, it will probably take the form of a solution that satisfies both you and the property owner. The chances of finding such an equitable solution are better if the property owner is an individual or a family as opposed to a development company. Why? Because the company acquired the property to develop it. Therefore, the development company may not be open to options that satisfy your concerns if those options fail to produce an adequate return on their investment. Nevertheless, your first step in searching for a quick victory should be a talk with the property owner, whether the owner is an individual, a family, or a development company.

If you cannot find a solution that is acceptable to you and the property owner, look at the land in question. Can it be developed? And, if so, will it be developed in a way that will adversely affect your interests? The best way to answer these questions is to meet with someone who is familiar with the property in question and who knows the requirements a development must meet in your area. You may find that these requirements will restrict the development in a manner that will protect your interests.

The final step in your search for a quick victory is to find out what the real estate market is like in the vicinity of the tract. Is there a demand for the type of development the owner plans for the property? Look for someone who is sympathetic to your position and who knows the local real estate market. This person should know if conditions favor the type of development envisioned by the owner. If the market is poor, development may not occur until conditions improve. At least you may learn how much time you have before the owner seriously pursues development of his property. You may even learn that market conditions are such that development is unlikely for quite some time.

MOTIVATIONS AND ATTITUDES

Throughout this book you will be encouraged to talk to government officials, development company executives, property owners, organization leaders, and a host of others. Some of these people may seem to be your natural adversaries; their goals, desires, and motivations are the opposite of yours. I urge you to avoid the temptation to think of these folks as bad people.

Over the past 20 years I have worked with hundreds of people who are involved in activities that affect neighborhoods and the environment. Yet I have never met a builder who wanted to pollute a stream, cause traffic congestion, or force an overcrowded school to accept more students. But, by the same token, I have never met a builder who shared my level of concern for clean water. And, not being a parent, I doubt that I could feel the same degree of concern for school conditions as the father of an eight-year old.

Builders, property owners, business executives, and government officials will have priorities that differ from yours. This does not mean that they are bad people. The reality is that a healthy economy is just as important as clean water. In fact, a case could be made that good schools, safe roads, and effective pollution control is dependent upon a robust economy.

If you adopt an attitude of mutual respect and acceptance, your dealings with others will be far more productive. The property owner has as much right to make a reasonable profit from the development of his land as you do from your occupation. If you condemn the owner or developer for putting profit before your values, you will be forced to fight for each concession.

WINNING THE PROPERTY OWNER'S SUPPORT

The purpose of meeting with the property owner is to:

- Let the owner know of your concerns;
- Find out what plans the owner has for the property;
- Determine if the owner is open to preserving the property in its current state;
- Look for a way to resolve your concerns that is compatible with the owner's development plans, if the owner intends to develop the property.

If you do not know who the owner is, contact the office in your city, township, county, or state that handles property tax assessments. The name and address of the property owner can usually be obtained from this office. If you run into difficulty, talk with a local real estate agent.

If you feel uneasy or uncertain about contacting the property owner, look for someone who can offer advice. Officials with your local planning agency or a land trust usually have extensive experience in negotiating with property owners. If your local government does not have a planning office, see if such an agency exists at the state level.

A land trust is a nonprofit organization that uses a variety of mechanisms to preserve land. You can locate land trusts in your area by contacting the Land Trust Exchange (see Appendix A). In fact, check with local land trusts, even if you do not feel you need help in dealing with the property owner. Who knows, you may find that you and the trust are interested in the same tract. By working jointly with the trust, the chances of satisfying your concerns will increase considerably.

If the property owner is a close friend of yours, or one of your allies, you can begin the negotiations quite informally by requesting a time when you can meet for coffee. But if this is not the case, make your first contact with the owner through a letter. End the letter with a request for a meeting and say that you will call in a few days to schedule an appointment.

The Letter

A letter is the best way to initiate your discussions with the property owner. The letter should be written in a concise, business-like manner. Never accuse, attack, or condemn the property owner. Instead, drawing from the exercises described in Chapter 2, state the potential damages that concern you, the benefits offered by the land in its present state, and any benefits you identified that might result from developing the tract. Make it clear that you hope to find a solution that is satisfactory to both you and owner. The letter should end with a request for an opportunity to meet with the owner to discuss the matter further.

If possible, the letter should be signed by someone that the property owner knows and respects. But do not let the question of who signs the letter hang you up. If the property owner wants to cooperate, the question of who signs the letter is a secondary matter.

Again, there is no need to make enemies at this point. Negotiations will proceed more smoothly if the discussion remains on a mature, business-like level. If the negotiations end with both sides agreeing to disagree, it will be easier to re-open discussions if conditions change in the future. If, on the other hand, you try to make the property owner feel like a bad person, the conversation will end abruptly. You will be forced to pull out all the stops in your campaign to deal with the development. So write the letter with the assumption that the owner has a legitimate right to benefit from his land, but that you want to let the owner know of your concerns.

An example of a letter to a property owner will be found on the following page.

The Phone Call

Place a call to the owner several days after your letter should have been received. Try to talk with the person your letter was addressed to. But do not be too surprised if you are referred to someone else, particularly if the letter was addressed to the head of a large company. Try to schedule a meeting with whoever has been designated to represent the property owner in discussions with you. You have nothing to lose by scheduling the meeting.

The Meeting

The meeting should proceed along the following general lines:
- Have the members of your party introduce themselves and state their interest in the property;
- Describe your goals and the basis for each (the damages to be avoided and the benefits you hope to preserve);
- Clearly state your desire to find a solution that satisfies you and allows the owner to make full use of his property;
- Ask the owner to describe his plans for the property (questions are suggested below for pursuing this point with the owner).

SAMPLE LETTER REQUESTING
A MEETING WITH A PROPERTY OWNER

Forest Hills Association
P.O. Box 333
Forest, MD 33333

February 18, 1989

Mrs. Elizabeth Hayes
1234 Woodland Drive
Forest, MD 33333

Dear Mrs. Hayes:

Several members of the Forest Hills Association and I would like an opportunity to talk with you about the 100-acre woodland you own, which adjoins our community. Many of the families residing in Forest Hills have long enjoyed the trout stream, the meadow, and natural beauty of the woodland. On behalf of the members of our association, I would like to thank you for allowing us to enjoy the woodland and for retaining this green space in a natural state.

I assume that at some point in the future you may consider developing the woodland. After all, it must be difficult to keep such a large tract of land in an unspoiled condition. We would like to explore how development may affect our community. Obviously, some disruption of the community is inevitable when the woodland is developed. But I am confident that we can find a way to minimize any disturbances to the community, while fostering the benefits that development may bring.

We would like to discuss several issues that may be affected by the development of the woodland. These issues are: school capacity, adequacy of wells, and the value of the stream and meadow as recreation areas.

I will call in a few days to discuss this request further.

Sincerely,

Judy Smithson,
President

If the owner is an individual, or a member of a family, pose the following questions to find out what plans exist for the property and what options there are for reaching a mutually satisfactory agreement.

- What plans does the owner have for the property?
- If development is being considered, try to find out why. It may be that property taxes have become unbearable. If this is the case, perhaps the owner can trade development rights for a lower tax rate. The chapter on land preservation describes methods for lowering property taxes by trading development rights.
- Would the owner be interested in preserving the tract in its present state? If so, see Chapter 4 for a discussion of the various options for land preservation.
- If the owner is sympathetic to your position, ask if he would be willing to place a covenant on the transfer of the property that would prevent potential damages to your interest and maintain the benefits the property currently offers.
- Look for ways in which you can help to achieve the owner's goals while, at the same time, attaining your goals.

If the property is owned by a development company, cover the following points during the meeting.

- What type of development does the company envision for the property?
- What would the company want to abandon the development venture? If the owner is willing to sell the property to a preservation agency, what is the asking price?
- Would the company agree to modify the development proposal in a way that would address your concerns?

If the property is still owned by an individual or family and they have hired a company to investigate development options for the site, try to meet with the owner, not a company representative. The owner is the person who ultimately decides how the property will be developed. It is better to talk directly with the owner yourself than to rely upon a development company official to do so. No one can present your case as well as you can.

At least two people should attend the meeting from your side, but there should be no more than six. One of your companions should take detailed notes of everything that is said, particularly by the owner. The purpose is to create an accurate record of what was said, such as the owner's statements about his plans for his property. Make certain that you understand the owner's wishes. An opportunity to attain your goals quickly may well turn on your interpretation of a single phrase. If any point seems vague, be sure to clarify it immediately. For instance, say "let me make certain that I understand you correctly. You would be willing to eliminate the house on the west side if. . . ."

The purpose of this meeting should be to gather information and pave the way for further discussions. Resist the temptation to come to any major points of agreement during the meeting; ask for a chance to think things over and to continue the discussion at some point in the future. Make certain, before the meeting, that all members of your party agree on this point.

Try to include in your group someone the owner knows and respects. In fact, mention this person by name in your letter requesting the meeting. This step will enhance your credibility with the owner. Examples of people the owner will respect include: the president of a local organization (particularly if the owner belongs to the group); an elected official (particularly one the owner supports, but does not control); a clergyman (particularly from the owner's church); a college or university president (particularly if the owner is an alumnus of the school); and anyone else who fits the general description reflected in these examples. But, make certain that the respected person supports your position 100 percent.

After the Meeting

Review the notes of the meeting with your supporters. Make certain that everyone agrees that the notes accurately reflect what was said during the meeting. Next, review your options.

If the owner does not plan to develop the property, is he open to preserving the land? If so, read Chapter 4—How to Preserve Land— and conduct the research described there to identify a suitable preservation option. If the owner is not planning to develop his property at this time and does not wish to consider preservation, complete the steps described in the next section of this chapter.

If the owner is committed to developing the property but is willing to consider modifying his plans to satisfy your concerns, continue the negotiating process. If the process is successful, protect your interests by: 1) asking the owner to sign a document that will legally bind him to your points of agreement, or 2) monitor the owner's development proposals by requesting copies of his plans or by checking with local development review officials. If the owner consents to signing an agreement, seek legal advice through the suggestions offered in Chapter 6. If negotiations reach an impasse or the owner does not adhere to an agreement, continue on to the next section of this chapter.

Finally, draft a letter to the owner thanking him/her for meeting with you and confirming your recollection of the major points of the meeting. You should also describe any steps you plan to take that may lead to a cooperative resolution of the issue. Say that you will be in touch with the owner once you have completed these steps.

HOW TO QUICKLY DETERMINE
IF THE SITE CAN BE DEVELOPED

Development constraints are factors that restrict the nature and extent of activities that may take place on a tract of land. A factor may constrain development either because it cannot be overcome without violating the law or the costs are too high.

Perhaps an example of a development constraint would be helpful. Homes constructed in rural areas usually rely on a well to satisfy household water needs. If an area is notorious for well failures, further development may be constrained due to the lack of a dependable water supply. The constraint may be reflected in a local development regulation prohibiting the construction of a home unless a satisfactory water source has been provided. It may be prohibitively expensive to pipe water in from some other source. Either way, development of the tract is constrained by the lack of an adequate water supply.

Development is generally regulated at the local level of government. Most counties, cities, towns, or boroughs have some process for reviewing proposed development ventures. The purpose of the review is to ensure that the project will not violate local laws designed to protect public health, safety, and welfare.

The sophistication of the development review process varies from jurisdiction to jurisdiction. Usually the most thorough review occurs in areas that are rapidly developing and relatively affluent. The review process may be virtually nonexistent in rural, impoverished areas in which local officials are desperately trying to attract development.

Keep in mind that the purpose of the review process is not to stop development projects, but to minimize adverse effects. In fact, the goal of most review officials is to find a way to make development ventures work with the least possible damage to public interests. It is an accepted fact that damage can never be eliminated. It is also generally accepted that the benefits of development frequently exceed these damages. While you may not agree with this philisophy, it is usually pointless to try to get a review official to help you kill a project. You will win greater cooperation from review officials if you are seen as someone who is looking for ways to address specific concerns, not for opportunities to block a development venture. Development review officials can be extremely powerful allies in your efforts to protect your interests. If an official agrees with your specific concerns, he may find ways of encouraging the property owner to seek satisfactory solutions.

To determine which unit of government reviews development proposals in your area, call the office of the mayor, town manager, county executive, or commissioners. Request an opportunity to meet with the head of the unit to discuss the property in question. Pose the following questions during the meeting:

1. How does the development review and approval process work?

   a. What requirements must a development proposal meet?

   b. What opportunities exist for public review and comment?

   c. What are the specific steps in the process, and how long does it take to complete each step?

2. Has the official received a development proposal for the property in question? If yes, what is the status of the proposal? Ask whether you can review the proposal. If the answer is no, ask what authority the official has for refusing you access to the proposal.

3. Are there any factors that would prevent development of the property?

4. If the answer to question 3, is No, then what type of development would be permitted on the site?

5. What factors may restrict development of the site?

   a. In what ways would development be restricted?

   b. How certain is it that the restrictions would be applied?

6. What factors have constrained development in the general vicinity of this site?

   a. Are these factors likely to apply to the site in question?

   b. How would development be limited by each factor?

   c. How certain is it that the restrictions would be applied?

   d. Who is responsible for enforcing the restrictions?

7. After describing your goals to the official, ask how he would proceed if he were in your position. For instance, if you are concerned about the effects of development upon a local waterway, ask what

steps the official would take to ensure the protection of the waterway. Who would he talk to? How would he investigate the question to learn what options are available for safeguarding aquatic resources? What review or permitting processes would he follow?

8. Finally, ask what approvals or permits may be needed if the property owner submits a development proposal. Find out what opportunities there will be for participating in the decisions concerning each approval or permit. Learn which decisions to grant a permit or approval can be appealed. The appeal process may provide an avenue for resolving specific issues, delaying development, or gaining negotiating leverage.

If the official says that it is quite unlikely that the property can be developed, then congratulations! It sounds like you just won a quick victory. But don't rest on your laurels. Check back with the official regularly. You may learn that someone found a way around the constraints. Also, go on to the next section of this chapter to see what the market is like for whatever development is permitted on the property. Market conditions will give you an idea of how energetically the owner might be in circumventing constraints.

If you did not find a "magic bullet"—one constraint that renders the site unsuitable for development—continue on to Chapter 5—Resolving Specific Development Issues—where you will learn how to research development constraints further. Additional research may uncover one or more constraints that will allow you to reach your goals. But before moving on to Chapter 5, use the suggestions offered in the next section of this chapter to look at the local real estate market.

WHAT DOES THE REAL ESTATE MARKET LOOK LIKE?

Development regulations are not written for the purpose of restricting changes in land use. The goal of development regulations is to ensure that the benefits of development are maximized while minimizing potential threats to public health, safety, and welfare. Therefore, it is quite rare that a tract of land is totally unfit for development. Something can always be built. The key question is Will that something be worth the expense involved in meeting local development regulations?

Perhaps the best person to help you answer this question is a real estate agent. Look for an agent who will speak with you openly. Discuss your goals and share the results of your conversation with the owner and the development review official. Ask for the agent's opinion on present and future demand for the type of development that may occur on the site.

Do not relax completely if you learn that market conditions discourage the type of development proposed by the owner. The owner may have other reasons for developing the tract that negate the problem of a poor market. For example, the owner may wish to build additional office space for his business. It may not matter that demand is poor for office space in your area. The owner may find it less costly to solve his office needs by building on his own land. Market conditions become most significant when the owner's primary motivation for development is profit, as opposed to fulfilling some other need.

If the owner is looking for a good return on his investment, a poor market may prompt a delay until conditions improve. You should use the time afforded by the delay to research development constraints further and to build your resources.

What if the owner is motivated by profit, yet market conditions are never likely to favor development of the site? Well, then, consider yourself lucky, but don't relax completely. Stay in touch with your market adviser to determine if conditions do change, despite his assurances. Also, check back with the development review official regularly to learn if the owner has submitted a proposal. Finally, it would be a good idea to research all potential development constraints to build the best case possible if a proposal is submitted.

You may wish to share your findings with the owner. The owner may have second thoughts about land preservation when he learns of all the factors impinging upon his wishes to develop the property.

Finally, if the owner states an asking price for the land, or is reluctant to name a figure, ask your real estate market expert how you might assess the value of the tract. The expert will probably look at adjacent lands that resemble the site in question and find out how much they sold for. In addition to the overall purchase price, find out what the profit margin has been on lands developed in the same manner as that proposed for your site. Perhaps the owner would agree to preserve the land, through a conservation easement or some other mechanism, if the owner were paid an amount equal to the profit derived from development plus the amount paid for the land.

4

How to
Preserve Land

The object of land preservation is to retain property in a totally or partially undeveloped state. There are four basic options for achieving this objective: acquisition, conservation easements, transfer of development rights or density (TDR), and a limited development venture (LDV). A number of other options may be available to a property owner interested in the tax benefits associated with land preservation. Such a property owner should contact the Land Trust Exchange (see Appendix A) or an attorney experienced in charitable gifts of real property.

The phrase "preservation entity" is used at various points throughout this chapter. The term refers to any agency, institution, or organization with the ability to utilize one of the four preservation options. A preservation entity will usually be a government agency, a land trust, or a foundation. But a preservation entity could also be one or more individuals with the resources to acquire a tract and retain it in an undeveloped state.

ACQUISITION

Land may be purchased by a government agency, a land trust, a foundation, citizen organizations, or by you and your supporters. Following are some suggestions for identifying those who may have interest in acquiring the land you hope to preserve. A list of questions is offered below to help you explore the potential for acquisition with each entity.

Government

Government agencies that may have interest in acquiring land include: local park departments, the National Park Service, and state natural resource, wildlife, and conservation agencies. You should begin your efforts to research preservation options with local agencies. Search for an agency official who seems sympathetic to your effort.

When you speak to government officials, ask if their powers of eminent domain can be used to acquire property if the owner refuses to sell. Although this is a drastic measure, it may well prove to be the lesser of evils if your relationship with the property owner becomes hostile.

Land Trusts

A land trust is a private, nonprofit organization that acquires land to preserve it for a specific use. Most land trusts only acquire tracts with certain characteristics, such as properties possessing unique ecological values, historical features, or having archeological significance. Other land trusts focus their resources within a specific geographical area. But a land trust can do more than acquire land. Land trust staff have extensive experience in negotiating with property owners and options for preserving land in addition to acquisition. As you begin your efforts to preserve a tract of land, contact the nearest land trust for advice. To learn about land trusts in your area, contact the Land Trust Exchange (see Appendix A). The folks at LTE can even help you form your own land trust.

Make an appointment to meet with the director of each local land trust to discuss your goals. Again, questions are offered below for getting the most out of your conversation with the land trust official.

Foundations

A few private foundations acquire land or make grants so others can preserve parcels for beneficial uses. The Foundation Center, a national nonprofit organization, publishes a directory of all the foundations in the United States. The directory, which is called, strangely enough, "The Foundation Directory," describes the criteria applicants must meet in order to be eligible for a grant from each foundation. To determine where you can review a copy of the directory, contact The Foundation Center (see Appendix A).

Using the directory, compile a list of foundations that have made grants for land acquisition in your area. Schedule an appointment with the director of each foundation. Cover the questions listed below during your conversation with the foundation executive.

Citizen Organizations

A number of citizen organizations acquire land. For instance, many bird-watching, conservation, and hunting-fishing clubs own land for use by their members. Some historical societies acquire buildings and adjacent lands. Your local library may have a listing of citizen groups in your area. Local elected officials may also know of groups in your area that acquire land. Talk with the president or director of each group to determine if they are interested in your tract.

You and Your Supporters

You should not rule out the possibility of raising the funds among your supporters to preserve all or a portion of a tract. It may even be possible to substantially lessen the impact of a proposed development venture simply by purchasing a few lots. In Chapter 8—Mobilizing Public Support for Your Cause—suggestions will be offered for raising funds. Land acquisition can be an exciting fund-raising theme. In fact, many people who refuse to donate funds for legal or political action will give generously for the purchase of land. And an aggressive grass-roots fund-raising effort has persuaded more than one local government into acquiring a tract they may have previously ignored.

Questions for Researching Land Acquisition Options

The following questions can be used to explore the ability of a preservation entity to acquire a tract of land.

1. What criteria does the organization use to determine which lands will be considered for acquisition?

2. Has the organization ever acquired land similar to the tract of interest to you?

3. Are there any factors that might prohibit the organization from applying its resources to the tract?

4. Who within the organization will participate in a decision concerning acquisition of the tract?

5. Which of the decision makers identified above are likely supporters or opponents? If a decision maker may oppose acquisition, find out why.

6. Would the organization consider a joint acquisition venture if another entity, such as a government agency, a foundation, or a land trust, shows interest?

7. What other organizations might have interest in acquiring the tract?

8. What are the probable limits of the organization's participation in an effort to acquire the tract?

9. If the organization is not presently inclined to apply its resources to your effort, what factors might cause it to reconsider?

10. What time constraints might be associated with the organization's participation in acquiring the tract?

Be certain to take careful notes throughout the entire discussion. In fact, you may wish to take someone along solely to record all that is said.

If you find an organization or agency that is interested in acquiring the tract, ask how the agency wishes to proceed. Does the agency's staff wish to approach the owner? Or should you first share what you have learned with the owner, then, if the owner expresses interest, schedule a meeting between agency representatives, the owner, and you? If a government agency has the ability to acquire the tract but is reluctant to do so, move on to Chapter 7—Encouraging Decision Makers to Support Your Cause. Chapter 7 will help you to plan your strategy for encouraging the agency to proceed with the acquisition of the tract.

If, on the other hand, acquisition seems highly improbable and you cannot foresee circumstances that might change the situation, you should read the next section on easements.

CONSERVATION EASEMENTS

A conservation easement is a legally binding agreement made between a property owner and a preservation entity, which is usually a government agency or a nonprofit organization. Through the easement, the owner agrees to forego certain uses of the land in exchange for other considerations, such as a reduction in income, estate, or property taxes, or a cash payment. While most easements are permanent, some have a shorter duration—from five to 25 years. The preservation entity that accepts the easement is also responsible for enforcing the terms of the agreement.

To locate easement programs in your area, call your local planning office, parks department, or the Land Trust Exchange (see Appendix

A; LTE has an excellent publication on this topic—"The Conservation Easement Handbook"). Contact each agency offering easements. Find out what requirements property owners must meet to participate in the program, the benefits derived by the owner, and the range of terms available through the easement program.

If you identify an easement program offering terms compatible with your goals that also meet the property owner's requirements, schedule a meeting between a representative of the easement program and the owner to begin the process of developing an agreement. If the owner eventually signs an easement agreement, go have a victory celebration.

If negotiations reach an impasse and the differences cannot be resolved, look for another easement program that may prove more attractive to the owner. If success remains elusive, perhaps the landowner would find one of the next two preservation options more appealing.

TRANSFER OF DENSITY/DEVELOPMENT RIGHTS (TDR)

Many local governments regulate the type and number of buildings that may be constructed on a parcel of land. Other characteristics of land use may be regulated as well. The transfer of density or development rights (TDR) has been used to preserve land in a totally or partially undeveloped condition. If an individual or company owns two tracts of land, within the same jurisdiction, the local government may allow the owner to transfer the uses permitted on one site to the other.

For example, let's say that a development company owns two tracts, each 100 acres in size. One tract is zoned for two houses per acre while the second can only accept one house per acre. So the "two houses per acre" tract can have a maximum of 200 houses, while 100 hundred homes can be built on the "one house per acre" parcel.

People residing in a community next to the "one house per acre" tract fear that development may cause excessive pollution or frequent traffic tie-ups. The local government agrees, but cannot afford to either improve the roads to accommodate more cars or install sophisticated equipment to control the anticipated pollution.

In this situation, the local bureaucracy may propose transferring the right to build 100 houses on the "one house per acre" tract to the other parcel. As a result, the number of houses that can be built on the "two houses per acre" site would increase from 200 to 300, while leaving the other tract in an undeveloped state.

Obviously, a transfer of density or development rights can be a very tricky technique to pull off. The local government must not only have the legal authority to make the transfer, but the willingness to do so as well. The owner must have another tract that can receive the density transfer, and people affected by development of the second tract must support the deal.

To find out if a TDR is an option, talk with someone in your local planning office. If local regulations permit a TDR, find out if the owner holds title to another tract of land in the area. If so, discuss the possibility of a TDR with the owner. If the owner is open to the idea, schedule a meeting between him and the appropriate official. If the TDR is still on track, read Chapter 6—Encouraging Decision Makers to Support Your Cause—for suggestions that will help make the TDR a reality.

If a TDR is not a viable solution, move on to the next and last preservation option.

LIMITED DEVELOPMENT VENTURE (LDV)

A limited development venture (LDV) can be used to preserve the best features of a tract by doing only enough building to pay for the cost of acquiring and preserving the tract.

For example, if the tract in question is 400 acres in size and the owner wants $10,000 an acre, the purchase price is $4 million. The organization or company wishing to preserve the majority of the tract may propose constructing 20 quarter-million dollar houses, on five-acre lots, for a gross return of $5 million. After subtracting development costs of $1 million (20 lots x $50,000/lot), the venture breaks even with a net of $4 million and only 100 of 300 acres are developed.

LDVs may be undertaken by land trusts, foundations, and some highly specialized development companies. Your local planning office may know of groups participating in LDVs. Contact the sources listed in Appendix A, under "Land Preservation," to locate land trusts or foundations involved in LDVs. Again, the virtue of this approach is that it provides income to the property owner while offering the hope of preserving the best portions of the site.

Once you locate an organization or company that participates in LDVs, find out if they might consider the land in question. If they are interested, ask what sort of development scheme they might pursue. If the scheme is compatible with your goals, get the property owner's reaction. If the owner is interested in the concept, schedule a meeting between you, the LDV company or organization, and the property owner.

Land preservation can be excruciatingly complex. Negotiating purchase price, easement terms, or partial development of a site frequently requires the services of a variety of skilled professionals. Again, as suggested repeatedly throughout this chapter, seek the guidance of people experienced with land preservation before charging ahead. Perhaps the best place to begin your search for advice is through a local land trust. The Land Trust Exchange (see Appendix A) can put you in touch with local sources of assistance.

There may be options for preserving land other than those described above. For example, if zoning is used to control development in your area, it may be possible to have a tract assigned to another zoning classification that markedly reduces or eliminates the development potential of the tract. Or it may be possible to modify development regulations in a manner that severely restricts certain activities or uses. To illustrate how this approach might work, let's say you are concerned about a tract that is quite hilly. In fact, many of the hillsides exceed a slope of 25 percent (the slope rises or falls 25 feet for every 100 feet of horizontal distance). Perhaps you can win passage of a change in development regulations that prohibits clearing, grading, and construction activity on slopes exceeding 25 percent. A victory may well render the site unfit for development.

If none of these preservation options will advance your goals and fulfill the property owner's needs, read Chapter 5—Resolving Specific Development Issues. If preservation is out, maybe you can satisfy your concerns through solutions addressing each specific damage or benefit identified in Chapter 2.

5

Resolving Specific Development Issues

A development issue may be any of the benefits or damages you iden-tified in Chapter 2. An issue may also include any other concern you have about the alteration of a particular tract of land or development in general.

Why should you attempt to resolve specific development issues? Well, if your concerns are "minor," it may be easier to solve a couple of issues as compared with the effort involved in launching a massive land preservation campaign. Or if your issues are major and land preservation is not a viable option, your only recourse is to seek solu-tions to each of your specific concerns. In rare cases, a site may be plagued by so many issues that the cost to resolve all concerns renders the tract unprofitable for development.

RESEARCHING DEVELOPMENT ISSUES

Research is the key to finding the best solution for each of your issues. There may be as many as a dozen potential ways to resolve a specific issue. Yet not all solutions will be equal. Some may not resolve the issue to your satisfaction. Other solutions may be unworkable because the property owner will not (or cannot) implement the solution, and no one has the authority to force implementation. The ideal solution is one that satisfies your concerns and can be implemented through minimal effort on your part. To begin your search for effective solu-tions, seek answers to the following questions.

1. *What solutions are available?* You can probably think of a number of potential solutions for each of your issues. But don't limit yourself to just a few ideas. Other solutions may be available that offer distinct advantages over those you initially listed. Generally, government is the best place to begin your search for solutions. Most development issues are studied, monitored, or regulated by some agency of government. Agency staff is frequently the best single source of information on a development issue. Many of the issues related to land development are described later in this chapter. Included with each description is a list of the government agencies that may help you to understand and resolve the development issue. To expand your list of solutions, contact the general information sources described below.

2. *Of these solutions, which do you prefer?* Your research will uncover a number of potential solutions for each issue. But which is the best solution? The answer to this question may depend upon the response to any or all of the following questions. To what degree will each solution prevent the damage or provide the benefit associated with an issue? Has the solution been previously applied successfully to situations similar to those associated with your issue? Under what conditions does the solution work best, and, if the solution has failed previously, what factors contributed to the failure? How long will the solution last? What sort of operation and maintenance difficulties might arise with each solution? How certain is it that adequate maintenance will be provided? What costs are associated with each solution, both initial and long-term? What undesirable side-effects may result from each solution?

While it is best to begin your search for a preferred solution with a government agency, do not stop there. Getting several opinions on each question is extremely important. It is unlikely that you will find one universally accepted answer to any question pertaining to a development issue. A developer, a government official, and your own expert may have widely differing opinions on just how effectively a particular solution will satisfy your concerns. Get the opinion of an expert who may be biased in your favor, such as someone who is also threatened by the issue. Or locate an advocacy group that is sympathetic to your position. For example, if you are concerned about water pollution, contact a local environmental group or a national advocacy organization such as the Sierra Club, the Audubon Society, Greenpeace, and so forth.

After considering all you have learned, rank each of your solutions from best to worst in terms of the degree to which each will satisfy your concerns.

3. *Who has the power to implement your preferred solutions?* Many people may have the power to implement a solution. A historic building can be preserved voluntarily by the owner. A regulatory agency might prohibit alteration of the structure. A parks department may purchase the building. An advocacy group could seek a court injunction to prevent the destruction of the historic property. A builder, who happens to be a history buff, could move the structure to another location. So there may be a number of individuals, agencies, institutions, or other entities with the power to implement a solution.

Again, government is the best place to begin your search for those who can implement a solution. When you meet with a government official to research solutions, ask who has the authority to implement each solution. If the agency cannot implement a solution to your satisfaction, request a copy of the laws, regulations, or policies the agency must follow. See if you can find a way to interpret these documents that would allow the agency to fully implement your preferred solution. Later, in Chapter 6—Do You Need A Lawyer?—you will learn how to confirm your suspicions about who has the legal authority to implement a solution. Be certain to ask about any approvals or permits that may be related to your issues. You may be able to gain crucial negotiating leverage by intervening in the issuance of a key permit or other approval needed by the property owner before development may proceed.

But, as always, do not end your research with the first government official you talk to. There may be more than one person who has the power to implement your preferred solution. Or, while government may have the power to act, it may be reluctant to do so because of some political concern. So continue your search for decision makers by contacting the information sources suggested below.

4. *Will decision maker(s) implement your preferred solutions?* How do you determine if a decision maker will implement a solution? Ask him.

If a solution is a simple, routine matter that is relatively inexpensive to implement, the decision may rest with one or two individuals. And these individuals may be easier to talk to than the highly placed decision makers presiding over solutions requiring vast sums of money. If your preferred solution is cheap and easy, it should be a simple matter to learn if decision makers will act as you wish.

Solutions that are expensive, such as land acquisition, may require the cooperation of many decision makers. To transform a proposed development site into parkland, you may need the support of a dozen decision makers ranging from the local parks department director, the county council, and the county executive, to the state parks agency and legislature. So as the magnitude of a solution grows, it becomes more difficult to determine how decision makers will act. And the answers you receive may be couched in less certain terms, such as "I may support the acquisition of the park if my constituents show strong support for the issue," or "Gee, I'd sure like to help you out, but I could only support the acquisition of your land if I can get support for the preservation of this other piece of property in my district."

Avoid the mistake of taking a "maybe" for a "no." A "maybe" could be a decision maker's way of asking for time to think about the solution before making a commitment. If a decision maker is genuinely undecided or weakly opposed, find out why. Perhaps you can swing the decision maker to your side. In Chapter 7—Encouraging Decision Makers to Support Your Cause—guidance will be provided for convincing decision makers to implement your preferred solutions.

Before making your own decision on a preferred solution, discuss what you have learned with others, particularly folks who have been active in dealing with development issues. They may see ways of interpreting your findings that produce dramatically different conclusions. A solution you had cast aside as hopeless may still be workable. The staff and leadership of advocacy groups can give you an informed, second opinion on your results.

In the end, your preferred solution may represent a compromise between the degree to which the solution resolves the issue and the effort required to convince decision makers to act. In other words, your preferred solution may satisfy most of your concerns, but not all, while necessitating something short of a Herculean effort to win the support of decision makers.

The following example will illustrate how research into a specific development issue might unfold.

An Example

Let's say that a community is concerned about a proposed development project. The project will greatly increase traffic flow on a road already plagued with rush-hour congestion and fender-bender accidents. Here's how the four research questions might be answered for this issue.

1. *What solutions are available?* Your talk with officials in your local highway and police department and the president of your neighborhood association revealed the following potential solutions:

- Improve traffic flow by installing better traffic control devices along the congested road;
- Divert traffic from the new development onto a less congested highway;
- Reduce congestion by adding more lanes to the existing road;
- Encourage car pooling;
- Ask major employers to stagger their hours of operation to reduce rush-hour congestion;
- Improve bus service and other mass transit facilities serving the area;
- Build a new highway;
- Allow the property owner to transfer his development rights to another tract where traffic congestion is not a problem;
- Postpone development until one or more of the above solutions can be implemented;
- Limit the size or type of development to reduce the number of cars added to the congested road;
- Prevent new development;
- Allow development to proceed and ignore the traffic problem.

2. *Of these solutions, which do you prefer?* While most of the solutions listed above have the potential for reducing traffic congestion, the degree of relief may range from barely noticeable to complete. In this case, the ideal solution should not only prevent traffic problems from becoming worse, but the solution should also relieve the existing congestion (as much as possible).

If you are not a traffic engineer, how do you tell which of these options may approach the definition of the ideal solution? Well, you should probably ask a traffic engineer, beginning perhaps with an expert in your local or state highway agency. But resist the temptation to settle for one expert's opinion. Instead, seek the opinion of several experts. At least one of these experts should have a perspective on the issue similar to yours, such as a traffic engineer who lives in the area and suffers the same rush-hour congestion you endure twice daily.

For the purpose of this example, we'll assume that you researched the traffic issue by contacting the following information sources: the director of the traffic engineering office of the local highway department; the commander of the traffic division of the police department; a professor in the planning department of the state university; the president of your local community association, who put you in touch with her counterpart in another group, which dealt with a similar issue two years ago; and a traffic expert with the state highway agency. From these conversations you learned that:

• Preventing new development would keep the situation from becoming worse, but would not improve existing conditions.

• Building a new superhighway is the only solution that will definitely solve traffic problems associated with existing and future development. Unfortunately, the highway is not only expensive, but may disrupt several adjacent neighborhoods.

• A combination of solutions may relieve traffic congestion now and for some time to come, but the number of options makes for a complex situation. In fact, the complexity is so great that no one can confidently predict just how much relief would be afforded. On the other hand, all of the options are relatively inexpensive to implement.

• While postponing or limiting development will prevent congestion from becoming worse, these options do little to improve the present situation.

• A transfer of development rights is unworkable because the property owner does not hold title to another tract that can receive the density.

• The last option, ignoring the problem, is rejected out-of-hand as a nonsolution.

After reviewing the information provided above, the preferred solutions are (from best to worst):

• Building a new highway, because it solves existing and future traffic problems;

• Combining the first six solutions, which also solves existing and future traffic congestion, but appears to be a less certain solution than a new highway;

• Postponing or limiting development may not help the present situation, but it does keep things from getting worse and should be easier to achieve than preventing development completely, and, finally,

• Preventing development appears to be the solution with the fewest benefits when compared to the effort required to implement the solution.

3. *Who has the power to implement your preferred solution?* The conversation with local and state highway officials revealed that the following decision makers must support the construction of the new road: the staff and director of the local and state highway agency, the county council and state legislature, and the county executive and governor. Additionally, those who own the property along the proposed highway alignment must agree to sell their land. If an owner refuses, a judge may become an additional decision maker as a result of court action to take the owner's property through condemnation. Also, elected officials will prefer the support of the leaders representing the neighborhoods affected by the highway. So there are many decision makers associated with this solution, each of whom may have the power to block implementation.

A number of decision makers are involved in the implementation of the first six solutions (improve traffic flow, divert traffic to a less congested road, widen the congested road, encourage car pooling, encourage employers to stagger working hours, and improve mass transit). The decision makers are: the staff and director of local and state highway agencies; several property owners; the county council and the state legislature; the county executive and governor; various employers; a bus company; a mass transit agency or other entities providing commuter services; and neighborhood association leaders.

Decision makers associated with an action to prevent, postpone, or limit development of the site are: the property owner and his development company; the local development review and approval bodies and, potentially, the county executive and county council; and a judge, if court action is necessary.

4. *Will decision maker(s) implement your preferred solution?* A new highway is a possibility. In fact, the chief of the planning division of the state highway department said that a new expressway has been proposed for the area. Unfortunately, the project may not be completed for another 10 years. But, the chief confided (off the record) that a strong showing of public support might accelerate the start of construction. After looking over the extensive list of power brokers associated with this issue, the decision was made to pursue other solutions for the time being.

Local highway officials said they were looking into ways of improving traffic flow along the congested road, but that, frankly, their ability to pursue this solution, along with encouraging car pooling and getting employers to stagger work hours, was quite limited due to the highway agency's limited manpower and budget. The officials felt they would have difficulty supporting a widening of the road. To add a new lane along both sides of the road, it would be necessary to demolish a number of residences—an expensive and politically difficult task. The officials did say that they would support diverting traffic from the proposed development to a less-congested road.

A talk with development review and approval officials revealed that the site resembles a number of other tracts recently approved in the same area. There does not appear to be any features unique to this site that might offer a legal or political argument to block, postpone, or limit development. The traffic issue alone is not sufficient cause to restrict development. Granted, most decision makers agree that traffic conditions are terrible, but how could they justify saying no to the development of the site in question when they approved so many other building projects in the immediate area? The officials did say that they would be open to the possibility of diverting traffic to a less congested street.

Given what the research has uncovered, the best solution might be to drop your opposition to the development if the owner agrees to divert traffic to a less congested highway. While this solution keeps conditions from growing worse, it does little to improve the unacceptable situation that presently exists. Therefore, a parallel campaign should be launched to support the efforts of the state to accelerate the construction of the new expressway.

In the final analysis, there is rarely one solution that is ideal from all perspectives. But your chances of finding the best solution increases as you learn more about each option. Research is, of course, the key to understanding each solution. To the extent that it is practical, you should tap each of the information sources described in the following sections until you run out of time and money.

GENERAL INFORMATION SOURCES

Following is a description of general sources of information. Later, in the section on specific development issues, suggestions will be offered for gathering information from sources unique to each issue.

Advocacy Organizations

Virtually every special interest group has some organization to protect its concerns. The organization watches for any action or trend that might threaten the interest group, such as proposed legislation, new regulations or policies, market shifts, or trends in public opinion.

Environmental groups, consumer organizations, and neighborhood associations are examples of special interest groups, each of which may serve as a valuable source of information on issues related to land development. The paid staff and officers of the organization can help you research issues related to their area of interest. For example, a highway agency may claim that little mud washes off their road construction sites to pollute nearby waterways. An environmental group may have learned that such claims are exaggerated. In fact, an investigation conducted by the environmental group revealed that mud pollution control is adequate only in a small percentage of the agency's construction sites. Therefore, if you are concerned about mud pollution, you should call for more effective control measures or push for a moratorium on further highway construction until the agency identifies and solves the problems that account for poor control.

How do you find special interest groups? The best way is to check with your representative in local and state legislative bodies. Most special interest groups spend a considerable amount of time tracking legislation. Your local councilman or state senator, delegate, or assemblyman can put you in touch with special interest groups that regularly contact his office.

The first group you talk to can then suggest other advocacy organizations that have the expertise you need. Leads on special interest groups may also be gained through the information desk at a local library, government agencies, the yellow pages of the phone book (check under "Associations"), newspaper reporters and editors, local chapters of national organizations (League of Women Voters, Sierra Club, etc.), church leaders, and the *Encyclopedia of Associations* (Gale Research, Inc., Book Tower, Detroit, MI 48226).

Computer Literature Search

How much development is too much? When and where should government allow a particular type of development? To what degree can control measures lessen the impacts of development? The answers to these questions are frequently based upon scientific research and other scholarly investigations. For example, a school board may base a limit on classroom size upon a study that showed that as the number of students per room exceeds a specific level test scores fall below the national average. The board may then propose a limit on further development in the service area of any school in which classroom size is nearing the critical threshold.

By examining research results pertaining to your issues, you can gain a better understanding of how a proposed development venture might affect you. From the scientific literature you can determine if proposed control measures will effectively protect your interests.

Today, a tremendous amount of information is stored in computer databases. A computer literature search allows you to scan each database to locate the specific information you need. You can access the latest findings on a given subject through "key words." For instance, you can get a listing of research papers on the water pollution impacts associated with highways by using the key words "highways," "water pollution," "roads," and so forth. The computer will generate a list of papers with these key words. You can usually decide which papers may be useful by scanning the titles. A full copy of each paper can then be obtained.

While there is nothing like a computer literature search for learning the "state-of-the-art" of a topic, this information source does have a few drawbacks. First, it can be expensive. Second, someone has to read and digest scholarly papers that may be full of terms so obscure as to confound even Mr. Webster. Third, the findings presented in the papers may be controversial and, if based upon studies performed elsewhere, may not directly apply to your situation.

But a literature search can be an extremely efficient way of identifying the leading experts in a specific field. And, even more importantly, the search may ease the task of locating experts with opinions favorable to your position. By scanning the literature, you can find out who is doing research in your field. When you locate an expert whose philosophy seems to conform to your own, note his name and place of employment and give the expert a call. Many researchers are quite willing to share their knowledge with people who are grappling with real-world problems. The researcher can help you to understand the issue and to determine if a proposed solution will work in your case.

Now that we've gotten the qualifying statements out of the way, let's get on with the use of a computer literature search. The first step is gaining access to the database. If you have a friend who owns a computer with a modem (a device that allows a computer to communicate over the telephone), ask the friend if he or she has access to a database. You can test the depth of your relationship by asking the friend to run a search for literature pertaining to your issue.

There are companies that conduct literature searches for those who lack a computer. For example, the National Technical Information Service (NTIS), a quasi-government entity based in Reston, Virginia, offers an excellent database retrieval service. The information desk at your local library can help you find other commercial information services. But be prepared for a fee that may run to $100 or more. So try your friends and supporters before shelling out a lot of money on a commercial database. Medical technicians, doctors, lawyers, corporate executives, college faculty, and any other professional may have access to a computer with the capability of performing a literature search, preferably at no cost to you.

Consultants

If you lack the time or inclination to become a lay expert on a development issue, you may wish to hire a consultant. Consultants tend to focus on specific areas of expertise. As a specialist, the consultant can keep up with the latest findings in his field. But consultants usually offer something far more important than just knowledge of the latest developments in the field—experience. By applying new findings to real-world problems, the consultant learns what works and what tends to fail. Combined, the knowledge and experience a consultant can offer will help you to separate solutions that merely seem to work from those that really will solve your problems.

Now that I have sold you on consultants, allow me to present the other side of the picture. Unfortunately, many consultants make their living servicing the development industry. Therefore, you may have difficulty finding a consultant who will agree to work for you, particularly if you are opposing a proposed development venture. And even if you do find someone who will take you on as a client, you may find that your expert tends to think more like the developer than you.

The ideal consultant not only supports your position, but has helped other people to successfully deal with an issue like yours. Such a consultant will spend fewer hours (and your dollars) educating himself on the issue. Whenever possible, use the consultant to review data or studies completed by someone else. It is less expensive to review someone else's work when compared to the cost of paying your consultant to collect and analyze data, then compile a report.

Always try to verify the conclusions reached by your consultant. Pose a sufficient number of probing questions to ensure that your consultant has fully thought out his conclusions. The consultant should give answers that are in plain language and make sense to you. If the consultant seems uncertain, confused, or takes offense at your questions, shop around for another expert.

The easiest way to find a good consultant is to talk to others who may use experts regularly, such as advocacy organizations. Consultants can also be found through the yellow pages in your phone book. Explain your needs to a number of consultants. Continue your search until you find someone who impresses you with his expertise and seems supportive of your position.

Corporations

Large corporations, utilities, or businesses may allow their experts to help you find effective solutions for your issues. Obviously, the more the corporation may benefit from your efforts, the more they will help you. For example, it may pay to contact businesses that compete with the company behind the development venture you are concerned about. In addition to offering the services of scientists, technicians, and other experts, a corporation may provide access to computer facilities and other services.

Design Manuals, Standards and Specifications, and Other Guides

Will it take a traffic light or a stop sign to provide an adequate degree of safety at an intersection? Do you need a large pond to capture mud washed from exposed, construction site soils, or will a row of straw bales form an effective barrier? These questions are frequently answered in the manuals, standards and specifications, and other guidance documents used by those who design development projects.

Surprisingly, many guidance documents are written in language most people can understand. From these publications you can gain a better understanding of the solutions available for each of your issues.

Guidance documents can be obtained through the government agency responsible for regulating each of your issues. The local highway department can tell you how to obtain design manuals and their standards and specifications for road construction. The state pollution control agency may have guidance publications on wetlands protection, stormwater management, or erosion and sediment control. Also, check to see if your local or college library has guidance documents on their shelves or the *Guide to Reference Books* (American Library Association).

Government Agencies

Generally, the best place to begin your research is with the government agency responsible for monitoring or regulating the activities associated with a development issue. If the issue pertains to on-site sewage disposal, contact the agency that issues permits for septic systems. When you are concerned about the type of use proposed for a site, schedule a meeting with the local zoning agency to determine if the use is permitted.

Find out what laws, regulations, or policies the property owner must meet. Ask for a copy of each and determine how much flexibility the agency has when enforcing these rules. If the agency would not normally enforce its rules to a point that would satisfy your concerns, ask if any language in their rules would prohibit more stringent enforcement. Subsequent chapters in this book will explain how to proceed if the agency feels it lacks the authority to resolve the issue to your satisfaction.

Frequently, more than one unit of government can provide information on a development issue. It is not uncommon for two agencies to share responsibility for an issue. For instance, the local planning office and highway department may jointly propose new road alignments. A state fisheries agency may recommend water quality standards for protecting sportfish, while the state pollution control agency enforces pollution discharge limits. Also, a federal agency may play an oversight or supporting role to a state agency, which in turn monitors a county or city agency. For example, the Federal Highway Administration sets many of the standards for road design and construction that state and local agencies must meet. A directory called *Information USA* (Viking Penguin Books) is an excellent reference for locating federal agencies that may provide information on your issue.

Once you have talked with the officials directly responsible for regulating the activities pertaining to your issue, ask what other local, state, or federal agencies may provide additional information. You may find that other levels of government have a different opinion on key aspects of your issue and the potential solutions. As you accumulate a greater variety of opinions, your understanding of the problem and your ability to identify the best solution will increase.

Finally, check with other jurisdictions, such as adjacent towns, counties, or states to learn how they deal with activities related to your issue. Other jurisdictions may have discovered better solutions than those used by your government officials.

Libraries

When in doubt, check with the information desk at your local library. You would be hard pressed to find a public servant who must respond to a wider variety of questions than a librarian. It is amazing how often a librarian can come up with an answer to questions about the most obscure topics. And even if the librarian does not get the precise information you need, at least she can point you in the right direction. Additionally, your local library may be a great storehouse of directories, such as the *Encyclopedia of Associations,* the directory of toll-free (800) numbers, product and manufacturer directories, and a host of others.

College and university libraries may carry professional journals and highly specialized publications pertaining to issues of concern to you. Most scientific and professional specialities have at least one journal in which the findings of recent studies or new techniques are published. For example, doctors have the *New England Journal of Medicine.* Land planners have the *Journal of the American Planning Association.* Pollution control specialists may refer to the *Journal of the Water Pollution Control Federation.* A browse through the periodical section of a college or university library may reveal several journals pertinent to your issue. The articles appearing in the journal will help you to better understand your issue and to find authors who may talk with you about potential solutions. But, this can be a time-consuming way to research an issue. Plus, you may find the technical jargon difficult to decipher.

Salespeople

What do you do when a developer boasts that your concerns about water quality impacts will be solved by the "Super-Duper Pollution Attentuator—Model B" he plans to use on his site? Well, you locate a company (through Thomas' Register) that sells a competing product. Then you place a call to their sales staff. As soon as you explain that you have a friend who's thinking of using a "Super-Duper Pollution Attentuator—Model B," the salesperson will tell you all the things that go wrong with his competition's product, then proceed to explain why you should buy his pollution attentuator. If you can separate the sales hype from fact, this option may be a valuable information source. Challenge the salesperson to support assertions with evidence. Is there proof that a Super-Duper Pollution Attentuator—Model B will not work in your situation? Ask for a copy of any studies the salesperson cited.

Sites Where a Solution Has Been Previously Applied

One way to judge just how effective a solution might be is to visit sites where the solution has been previously applied. Hopefully the site will resemble the property in question. And, if you get real lucky, the solution will have been implemented by the same people that will execute the solution on your site. Should you find yourself in this enviable position, you can judge just how well the solution has worked. Be certain to talk to people who live near the site to learn of any of the less obvious problems with the solution. The neighbors can tell if the "Super-Duper Pollution Attentuator—Model B" really is odorless, quiet, and releases a "drinking-water" quality effluent into the nearest waterway.

Trade or Professional Associations

Most scientific, professional, or skilled employment fields are represented by an association. Examples include the American Medical Association, the American Fisheries Society, or the American Society of Civil Engineers. A number of trade and professional associations have staff experts who will answer questions related to their specialty. Also, the association can refer you to members in your area who have the expertise and perspective you are looking for. Many local libraries carry the *Encyclopedia of Associations* (Gale Research, Inc., Book Tower, Detroit, Mich. 48226).

University and College Faculty

A professor or instructor with a nearby college or university may provide expert advice on issues of concern to you. The faculty at these institutions are often familiar with the latest findings concerning an issue. This information can be extremely important to your efforts to find the best solution for your issue.

You should begin your search for experts at the office of the chairman of the appropriate department. For instance, if you feel that a site may harbor an endangered species of plant or animal life, contact the chairman of the Biology Department. An expert on stormwater management might be found through the office of the chairman of the

Department of Civil Engineering. Or the information desk at the institution's library may offer leads.

Your Supporters

Look to the folks who actively support your efforts as a source of information and help in conducting research. Divide up research responsibilities among your supporters. Also, make certain that each of your supporters knows of the specific information you are seeking. One person may volunteer his computer and modem for a literature search, while another may offer to review and summarize the results. A third person may ask his boss, a geologist, for his opinion on the effects of a development upon nearby wells. You may find a variety of skills and professions represented among your supporters, such as accountants, attorneys, doctors, engineers, and so forth.

DEVELOPMENT ISSUES

Following is a summary of the issues that may be associated with a land development venture. A brief description is offered for each issue along with potential information sources. Additional sources of information may be found in Appendix A.

Archeological or Historic Features

A feature with archeological or historic significance may include a Native American burial site or village, a building that is quite old or was once the home of a famous person, or an industrial site representing a bygone era. A feature need not be located on the premises to affect the development potential of a site. Restrictions may be applied to development taking place on property adjoining an important feature.

If you suspect that an archeological or historic feature exists on or near the proposed development site, check with your local and state government offices, many of which have inventoried sites within their boundaries. Other sources of information may include historical societies, the social studies department of the nearest college or university, or Native American groups in your area.

Aquatic Resources

Are there any unique or valued aquatic resources located either on or downstream of the proposed development site? Examples of unique or valued resources include waters highly regarded by sportfishermen, water supply reservoirs, waters supporting an endangered species, and areas heavily used for boating or swimming.

Look at the factors that may affect the quality of aquatic resources, such as buffers, flooding, septic systems, sewerlines, soil erosion, stormwater management, and wetlands. When examining each factor determine if the development can meet criteria intended to protect each important aquatic resource. Take a close look at the criteria as well. Are the criteria adequate to fully protect the resource? The following government agencies can assist you in protecting important aquatic resources: your state environmental protection and fisheries management agency, the U.S. Fish and Wildlife Service (an agency of the U.S. Department of Interior), and the regional office of the U.S. Environmental Protection Agency.

Buffers

A buffer is intended to protect a valued feature from a potential threat. Some jurisdictions require a buffer between noisy roads and nearby homes. Others call for a dense buffer of trees and shrubs along waterways. A buffer can also be used to create a transition zone between incompatible land uses, such as residential and industrial areas.

Like all protection measures, a buffer will rarely eliminate a threat. At best, it reduces the impact to a tolerable level, however subjectively "tolerable" may be defined. In addition to protecting adjacent features, buffers also reduce the amount of land available for development, which tends to further offset impacts.

The U.S. Fish and Wildlife Service and your state fisheries management agency can provide information on buffers for protecting aquatic resources. The Federal Highway Administration and your state or local highway agencies can explain how road noise can be buffered. Planning agencies and architectural associations can offer guidance on the use of buffers to soften the impact of conflicting land uses.

Dangerous Sites

Some lands are unsuitable for development because of natural or man-made factors that threaten public health, safety, or welfare. Examples may include sites located in areas prone to earthquakes, land subsidence, or flooding. Properties located on or near abandoned landfills or mining sites may be contaminated with materials hazardous to human health. Quarries frequently have deep pits that may pose a danger due to drowning or falling.

In some cases, development may offer the benefit of eliminating a danger, such as filling in an abandoned quarry pit. In other situations, development should be postponed until the danger can be removed (if possible). Had this philosophy been followed in New York state, we would not associate the name Love Canal with terms such as hazardous waste, cancer, miscarriages, and evacuation.

Frequently, people who live near a development site will know of any dangers associated with the property. Your local office of the U.S. Geological Survey may know of areas prone to earthquakes, sinkholes, and other natural dangers. The state environmental agency or the regional office of the U.S. Environmental Protection Agency will know of landfills, hazardous waste sites, and other contaminated areas. The regional office of the Federal Emergency Management Agency may know of other dangers present in the vicinity of a proposed development site.

Deed Restrictions

Occasionally, a deed will contain restrictions on the type of uses that may occur on a tract of land. For instance, at one time someone may have owned the land who enjoyed its scenic qualities. Or, perhaps a past owner saw his land as a haven for wildlife. In either case, the owner may have sold the land with the understanding that it would be retained in an undeveloped state. This understanding may have been written into a deed in the form of language restricting development of the site.

Talk to people who know the history of the land; ask about previous owners. If you have any reason to believe that some prior deed may carry a restriction, have a title search performed. For a few hundred dollars, a lawyer or a title company can research a deed to determine if any unusual restrictions exist on the use of the property. Granted, this is a long shot, but sometimes it does pay off.

Also, take a look at access to roads. Does the property front on a road with sufficient capacity to accommodate the traffic that may result from development? If a tract is separated from a road by property owned by another, access may be severely limited unless a right-of-way can be acquired. Again, if you feel access may be a problem, have a competent attorney research the question for you.

Endangered Species

The U.S. Fish and Wildlife Service is responsible for designating and protecting endangered plants, fish, mammals, and other wildlife. A number of states have designated additional species that are endangered within their boundaries. An endangered species may not preclude development of a site. Instead, the owner may be required to set aside a portion of the site to protect the species. Also, more stringent pollution control measures may be required. Contact the nearest office of the U.S. Fish and Wildlife Service (USFWS) for information on endangered species. The USFWS can tell you which agency oversees endangered species in your state.

Farmland Preservation

The loss of prime, productive farmland to other uses is diminishing our ability to grow sufficient quantities of food and other agricultural products. Programs have been started throughout the nation to slow the rate of loss. If the tract in question consists of prime, productive farmland, research options for preserving the site by contacting your local office of the U.S. Department of Agriculture, the Agricultural Stabilization and Conservation Service, or the Soil Conservation Service. The staff serving each of these agencies will know of farmland preservation efforts in your area. Further information may be obtained through associations such as the Grange, the farm bureau, 4-H, a state agricultural agency, or the cooperative extension service associated with your state university.

Flooding

Converting forest or farms to lawn, concrete, and asphalt increases stormwater runoff and downstream flooding. In fact, development can increase the frequency and severity of flooding a hundredfold! Most review agencies analyze the floodwater impact of proposed development projects. If the project will increase the threat of flooding at downstream homes, bridges, or other structures, control measures must be used.

Take a look at the waterways that will receive runoff from the proposed development. Are there homes, businesses, or other properties located downstream that have suffered flood damage in the past? If the answer is yes, then increases in stormwater runoff, as a result of development, must be strictly controlled. If you have difficulty answering this question, contact your state coordinator for the National Flood Insurance Program, which is administered by the Federal Emergency Management Agency.

Computing stormwater runoff and floodwater elevations is not an exact science. There is a substantial margin of error in both the estimates of runoff quantity and the effectiveness of flood-control measures. Ask for the data used by the review agency to evaluate flood impacts from the proposed development. Also, request a copy of information pertaining to any flood-control measures associated with the project. Obtain the services of a hydrologist, a civil engineer, or some other person skilled in floodwater estimation and control. Ask the expert to assess the accuracy of the flood estimates. Also, have the expert make a worst-case estimate of the flooding impacts that might result from the development. Finally, take a look at the flooding that might result if all surrounding lands were developed. The cumulative flood effects of all future development may prove quite startling.

A development project must not increase the potential for floodwater damage to downstream properties. If the risk cannot be eliminated through control measures, the project should either be scaled down or prohibited.

Noise

Some jurisdictions require an analysis of noise associated with development proposals. Many highway projects must perform an analysis of noise impacts. The project may be severely constrained if noise standards will be exceeded. Particularly stringent restrictions may be imposed if noise standards are already exceeded in the vicinity of a proposed development. Contact your local and state highway or public health agencies for further information on this topic. Other sources of information include the Federal Highway Administration, the U.S. Urban Mass Transportation Administration, and the U.S. Environmental Protection Agency.

Property Value

The value of a home can be affected by adjacent dwellings. The same may hold true for new development constructed next to an established neighborhood. The difference in selling price may raise or lower the value of the existing homes. An increase in home value can lead to a rise in property taxes, which may impose a financial hardship on homeowners living on fixed incomes. A decline in home re-sale value will lower the equity the owner has accumulated.

While a specific review agency may not have the responsibility for considering this impact, that does not mean the issue cannot be raised. Countermeasures may include the construction of a "buffer" of equally priced homes along the border with the established community. Or freezing property assessment rates at the pre-development level.

Schools

Education is an issue the public is particularly sensitive to; only traffic congestion generates greater public outcry. The quality of a child's education is related, in part, to class size. As class size increases, teachers spend less time helping individual students. Expanding student enrollment becomes critical when school capacity is exceeded. These factors combine to lower the quality of each student's education.

Most school systems develop projections of future student enrollment. If a school is at or near capacity, further development within the service area can only worsen the problem. Development should be postponed until additional capacity can be provided. Your local teacher's union or association may be a good source of guidance on this topic. Also, check with the PTA for schools that may receive students from the proposed development project. Other sources of information include the local school board and state education department.

Septic Systems

A septic system is used to dispose of household wastewaters in areas far removed from a sewerline. Toilet, sink, and laundry water flows to a septic tank where solids settle out. The liquid then flows to pipes or pits that allow wastewater to soak into surrounding soils. But not all soils are suitable for septic systems. In fact, poor soil conditions is a primary factor restricting development in rural areas.

Take a look at existing development about the land you are interested in. Look for signs of septic system failure, such as portions of the lawn that stay wet most of the time, the presence of sewage in ditches or nearby streams, or the frequent appearance of septic tank cleaners in the neighborhood. Also, your local health department will have records of septic system failures.

A failing septic system releases poorly treated sewage into the environment. The sewage may contaminate wells or streams and result in disease and pollution. If an area has a history of septic system failures, further development should be restricted. The restriction should continue until the cause of the high failure rate is identified and realistic corrective measures are instituted.

Sewerlines

Sanitary sewerlines carry household wastewaters to a sewage treatment plant. The sewerline consists of a system of iron, concrete, or plastic pipes, which utilize gravity to carry sewage downstream to the treatment plant. The smallest pipes connect to each house, join a larger pipe serving a block of homes, which combines with still-larger sewers receiving wastewater from an entire neighborhood or community. Eventually, the sewer will run parallel to a stream, where an abrupt release of sewage will result in water pollution.

A sewerline does not have an unlimited capacity to carry sewage. Each home connected to a sewer may add another 350 gallons of sewage per day. As more homes are connected to a sewer, the capacity diminishes. If connections continue, despite diminishing capacity, the sewer will become overloaded and sewage overflows will grow increasingly common.

Additional connections, whether residential, commercial, or industrial should not be allowed if a sewer is at or over its rated capacity. Check with local public works and health officials to determine how much capacity remains in the sewer serving the site in question. Ask for a copy of the study supporting their estimate of the remaining capacity. If the accuracy of the capacity estimates seem questionable, find a competent expert to conduct an independent review.

Find out how frequently sewage escapes from the sewer, particularly at pumping and lift stations. Frequent sewage releases can occur even if a sewerline is well below capacity. If sewage releases are common, additional connections should not be allowed until the cause of the problem is corrected. Also, check to see how much capacity remains at the sewage treatment plant. Find out how frequently the plant violates its discharge permit. Contact your regional office of the U.S. Environmental Protection Agency to learn who regulates discharge permits in your area.

In summary, you can make a strong case for prohibiting further development in an area served by a sewerline if sewage overflows occur presently, particularly if the sewer is at or over capacity or a lack of maintenance has allowed the sewer or pumping stations to deteriorate. Further development should also be prohibited if the sewage treatment plant fails to meet the pollution control limits contained in the discharge permit issued to the facility.

Soil Erosion

During the construction phase of development, erosion on each acre of barren soil can release more than 100 tons of mud into nearby waterways. The mud pollution from the average construction site may damage three miles of waterway and recovery can take up to a century.

In a number of jurisdictions across the nation, builders are required to use ponds and other measures to trap mud on construction sites. Check to see if builders in your area are required to use these erosion and sediment control practices. If not, development of your site may result in substantial pollution of downstream areas. If the site will affect an important aquatic resource, development should not occur until proper protection measures can be incorporated into construction plans.

Even in areas where erosion and sediment control is required, only 25 percent of all builders may make full use of control measures. If control quality is equally poor in your area, development should be restricted until the situation improves.

Finally, some soils and sites will generate more eroded soil than others. Development should not occur on the most erodible soils in an area. If your site is composed of erosion-susceptible soils, it may be possible to shift development to some other area.

For further information on erosion and sediment control, contact your local public works or health agency, your state environmental protection office, the U.S. Soil Conservation Service, or the U.S. Environmental Protection Agency.

Steep Slopes

Development of steep slopes may lead to a number of problems. Fire trucks and other emergency vehicles have difficulty ascending roads constructed on a steep grade. As slope steepness increases, so does the potential for soil erosion. Septic system drain fields may not function properly on steep slopes. Finally, it is difficult to operate mowers and other heavy equipment safely on steep slopes.

Across the nation many development review agencies restrict building activities on slopes steeper than 15 percent to 25 percent. A

15 percent slopes rises or falls 15 feet for every 100 feet of horizontal distance. If slopes on your site exceed 15 percent, determine if your local review agency regulates steep-slope development. If the answer is yes, find out what restrictions apply to steep slopes and the rationale supporting the restrictions. If you can demonstrate that the current restrictions are not sufficient, you may succeed in winning tighter controls on your site. If the review agency does not regulate steep slope development, consider a campaign to make your site the first to benefit from steep slope protection.

Stormwater Runoff

The quality and quantity of rainwater runoff changes dramatically when rural land is converted to homes, lawns, streets, and parking lots. Downstream flooding can increase a hundredfold and runoff may contain as much pollution as untreated sewage! Generally, stormwater runoff will first begin damaging downstream areas when the land draining to a waterway has more than one home for every two acres. Waterways die when the density reaches one home per half acre.

Stormwater management measures, such as ponds, stone-filled infiltration trenches, and grassed waterways may reduce runoff impacts to a tolerable level. Determine if stormwater control will be required on your site. If not, important aquatic resources may be severely damaged. Development should not occur until a commitment is made to use adequate control measures. If stormwater control is required, determine if the mitigation measures will reduce runoff impacts sufficiently to protect aquatic resources. Biologists with your state fisheries management agency may be familiar with stormwater impacts and the level of control needed to protect sportfish.

It is difficult to find a stream in the U.S. that does not eventually enter some other waterway serving as a source of drinking water. Stormwater runoff from developed lands contains a number of pollutants that lower the quality of drinking water. Development should not occur in areas that drain to water supply sources unless pollutant levels can be reduced sufficiently to meet drinking water standards.

Additional information on stormwater management may be obtained from your local public works or health department, a state natural resources or environmental protection agency, the U.S. Soil Conservation Service, or the U.S. Environmental Protection Agency.

Traffic

Of all the impacts associated with development, traffic problems cause the greatest public concern. When road improvements fail to keep pace with development, traffic congestion and accidents escalate.

Most review agencies will use a standard formula for calculating the additional traffic generated by a proposed development. For instance, a single-family dwelling may generate eight to 12 additional car trips per day. Some local highway departments set an upper limit on the amount of traffic a road can handle. Once development generates sufficient traffic to reach the limit, further building must await steps to increase road capacity.

Determine what criteria local review agencies use to regulate traffic increases. Find out what the basis is for the criteria, particularly the degree of public safety afforded by the criteria. Ask what the remaining capacity is for roads affected by the proposed development.

If the streets serving a proposed development are well known for traffic jams or frequent accidents, carefully research this potential constraint. Try to obtain information on the frequency of accidents and how the frequency has changed with more development. Consider the cumulative impact resulting from the development of all vacant lands affecting the street, not just your site. The total impact may be quite alarming. You may find public sentiment already in your favor if you propose limiting further development along streets notorious for traffic problems.

For information on traffic concerns, contact your local highway or planning office, your state highway agency, or the Federal Highway Administration.

Water Supply

Water for drinking, washing, or commercial uses may be obtained from wells, a water supply reservoir, or drawn directly from a river. Any water supply source can be depleted if a limit is not placed on the number of homes and businesses drawing upon the source.

Find out what source will be used to provide water for the proposed development. If groundwater will be tapped through wells, ask what criteria will be used to verify the adequacy of the wells. Find out if well failures are common in the vicinity of your site. Development should not occur until the cause of well failures is determined and steps are taken to ensure that similar problems do not occur on your site.

If the development will be served by water drawn from a reservoir or river, determine the status of the source of supply. Ask if a limit has been established for water withdrawals. If such a limit has been established, ask how much capacity remains. If a limit has not been established, talk with local personnel of the U.S. Geological Survey, an agency of the Department of Interior. Ask what data they have on the quantity of water available from the source and the effects of water withdrawals.

If water rationing or use restrictions have been imposed in your area, the supply must be near the limit, at least during drought periods. The more severe the restrictions, the worse the situation is. If your area is prone to water shortages, or the supply is nearing an upper limit, further development should be curtailed until the water supply is increased.

Wetlands

Swamps, bogs, marshes, and tidal flats are all examples of wetlands. A wetland is a vital component of aquatic ecosystems. Wetlands neutralize pollutants and provide food and cover for aquatic creatures. Agriculture and development activities have destroyed thousands of acres of wetlands throughout the nation. Though the rate of loss has slowed, wetlands continue to decline at an alarming pace.

The U.S. Army Corps of Engineers regulates wetland alterations through a permitting process known as "404," named after a section of the federal Clean Water Act. Many states have their own wetland permitting activities to augment the 404 program.

The U.S. Fish and Wildlife Service (USFWS) has cataloged wetlands throughout the country. Check with your local USFWS office to determine if wetlands occur on your site. Also, local or state agencies may operate wetland protection programs. The USFWS should know of programs in your area. Check with the local programs to learn of additional opportunities to protect wetlands.

A 404 permit or other approvals may be needed if a developer intends to use heavy equipment in the vicinity of streams, rivers, floodplains, ponds, swamps, marshes, bogs, or any other area that is wet for all or part of the year. Let review agencies know if a wetland occurs on the site. Find out what steps they will take to protect the wetland and what opportunities you have to participate in permitting decisions. With the 404 program, substantial opportunities exist for citizen involvement.

Zoning and Master Plans

Zoning is employed in many areas of the nation to regulate the density and type of uses that may occur on a parcel of land. If zoning is used to guide land use in your area, take a close look at the designation for the site in question. Does zoning permit uses on the site that may affect your interests? If so, explore the possibility of changing the zoning designation for the tract. Determine if the proposed development project is consistent with a strict interpretation of the uses permitted by zoning regulations. If the zoning criteria permit a use that you feel is a threat to public health, safety, or welfare, consider a campaign to change the criteria. Chapter 11—Dealing With Development on a Community Level—offers guidance on launching a campaign to change development regulations and zoning laws.

A master plan (or comprehensive plan) serves as a general guide for land use throughout a township, borough, or county. Take a look at the plan to learn what uses are called for in the vicinity of the site in question. Development ventures have been constrained when the proposed use conflicted with the master plan, even when the use was permitted by the zoning regulations.

Information on zoning and other land use controls may be obtained from your local planning and zoning office or a state land planning agency. Further information may be obtained from the sources listed in Appendix A, under the heading of "Land Preservation," or the American Planning Association.

SUMMARIZE YOUR FINDINGS

Keep a written record of all you learn as you research each issue. Your written record will ensure that key points are not forgotten. Or that solutions for one issue are not confused with another.

As you complete your research for each issue, summarize your findings. Suggestions will be offered in subsequent chapters of this book for using the summary to acquaint others with opportunities to resolve each issue. The summary may be particularly valuable in your efforts to find a competent attorney, to win the support of decision makers, and to mobilize public support for your cause. Be certain to address each of the four research questions suggested at the beginning of this chapter.

WHERE DO YOU GO FROM HERE?

Based upon the summary of your findings, is there a solution or a combination of solutions, that will resolve each issue to your satisfaction?

If the answer is no, and land preservation is not an option, reconsider your definition of an acceptable solution. Is the definition realistic? Could it be modified without posing an unacceptable threat to your interests? If you still feel your definition is realistic and should not be modified, go on to Chapter 6—Do You Need a Lawyer? Perhaps an attorney can find an opportunity for satisfactorily resolving each issue.

If the position of decision makers on a solution is uncertain or if they do not plan to apply the solution to your satisfaction, move on to Chapter 6—Do You Need a Lawyer?—and Chapter 7—Encouraging Decision Makers to Support Your Cause. Perhaps you can find opportunities to constrain development of the site that would then give you the negotiating leverage needed to convince the property owner to implement your preferred solution.

If you identified a solution(s) that will resolve each issue to your satisfaction, will decision makers implement the solution? If the answer is yes, it sounds like victory is yours. But, just to be on the safe side, read the remainder of this book. You may find ideas that will further solidify success.

CHAPTER

6

Do You Need
a Lawyer?

There is a response that people commonly have when they first hear of a development proposal. They immediately run out and hire a lawyer to stop the project. Frequently, this reaction seems to be more a product of reflex than logic because legal action seldom results in killing a development venture.

Purchasing land and preparing a development proposal is expensive. Few property owners will spend all this money unless they feel the proposal has a good chance of gaining all the approvals and permits needed from government. An attorney can only succeed in killing a project if it violates some development regulation or fails to qualify for an essential permit. And even if the attorney finds a fatal flaw, the owner may then simply modify his proposal to circumvent the problem. Nevertheless, there are those rare proposals that contain an incurable defect, for legal action does occasionally succeed in striking a deadly blow to a development venture.

Delay is a far more likely outcome of legal action. It is frequently possible to use the law to interfere with and stall the owner's attempts to receive the approvals and permits needed to begin development. Through delay, you can drive up the owner's costs, which may increase his willingness to negotiate with you, assuming, of course, that you are interested in concessions such as fewer lots, preserving a portion of the tract, lowering the purchase price if you are seeking acquisition by a preservation entity, or some other solution that may satisfy you. Also, it may be possible to use delay to drive up development costs to the point where the owner is forced to abandon the venture. But, generally, the more extreme your goal, the less likely it will be that delay will allow you to attain your goal. In other words, it is more likely that delay will prompt the owner to sacrifice 10 percent of his tract rather then forcing him to abandon the proposal completely.

All this discussion of legal action, and what a lawyer may or may not do for you, has been offered to help you see the need for defining your goals realistically. Once you know what you want to accomplish, it will be easier to find the best legal strategy and lawyer to help you attain your goals. If you hope to use the law to kill a development proposal, the best legal strategy is one that has succeeded in killing other development proposals. If you cannot find an attorney who has defeated a development venture in the past, this may be an unrealistic goal given the development regulations and judicial/political atmosphere in your part of the world. This does not mean that you should abandon your goal of killing a proposal. What it does mean is that the chances of success may not be very good.

The most dependable method for finding the best legal strategy and lawyer to help you attain your goals is to shop around. The following suggestions will help you in your search for competent legal representation.

CHOOSING A LAWYER

Begin your search by compiling a list of attorneys who have experience helping others to protect their interests from the damages associated with development. Contact advocacy groups, both local and national, and others who have been active in dealing with land preservation and development issues in your area. Ask if they know of any attorneys who make a habit of representing clients concerned about a proposed development project. Also, ask about attorneys who help citizen groups with related issues, such as social justice causes, the environment, and so forth. If you have difficulty locating attorneys, check with the lawyer referral services operated by groups such as the American Bar Association. Contact your public library or county law library and ask if they have a directory of lawyers, such as the reference distributed by Martindale-Hubbell, Inc., of Summit, New Jersey. This directory lists all the attorneys in the nation and rates their ability and reputation. Generally, you should avoid attorneys who specialize in helping property owners to develop their land.

Once you have compiled a list of attorneys, prepare a summary of your concerns and the results of your research. Begin the summary with a description of the property and a statement of your goals, along with the specific damages you hope to prevent and the benefits you seek to perpetuate. Next, describe the results of your conversation with the property owner. Discuss any land preservation options that may still be open for consideration. Attach a copy of the write-up you prepared after researching solutions for specific development issues. Be certain to mention each approval or permit the property owner may need to develop his land. Describe any development proposals that have been made for the property.

Once you have prepared the issue summary, you are ready to begin interviewing attorneys. That's right. You are going to shop for a lawyer who can not only propose the best strategy for protecting your interests, but who can do the job at a price you can afford. Attach a cover letter to the description, and mail it to each attorney. Make it clear that you are shopping for an attorney who can propose a plausible strategy for winning the issue.

When you talk with each attorney, pose an open-ended question that encourages the attorney to explain how he would pursue your issue. If it is obvious that the attorney has not read the issue summary, cut the conversation short and go on to the next attorney. Following are several points to consider when evaluating attorneys.

1. Explanations should be given in clear, understandable language, and the attorney should respond in an open, courteous way to your questions. Avoid attorneys who talk down to you, act in a patronizing way, or expect you to accept what they say without question.

2. Does the strategy proposed by the attorney make sense to you? The attorney should describe the specific steps he will take, why he proposes to take each step, and what might be gained from each step.

3. If the attorney feels he does not know enough to propose a strategy, ask him to describe what steps he will take to learn more about the issue. Do these steps sound reasonable to you?

4. The attorney should give an estimate of your overall chance of success. If he feels he cannot make a projection now, ask at what point an estimate can be made.

5. Ask what his fee will be, how much he wants to start work (a retainer), and what the case may ultimately cost.

6. Make certain that neither he nor any other attorney in his law firm represents the property owner or the development company on other matters.

7. Finally, ask at what point you should bring an attorney into the case. If a hearing is coming up, ask if you really need legal counsel at the hearing. If the answer is yes, ask for specific reasons why an attorney is necessary.

After you have interviewed several attorneys, review the results of each conversation. If one attorney's explanation conflicts with another, talk to both attorneys again, describe the conflicting information, and ask for a clarification. The response you get may be quite helpful in selecting the most competent attorney.

Avoid the temptation to go with the cheapest attorney. You tend to get what you pay for. In Chapter 8—Mobilizing Support for Your Cause—you will learn how to estimate the amount of financial support available to your effort. Rather then settling for second best, take another look at your fund-raising position and see if you can go for number one. Finally, never try to get attorneys into a bidding war. You may end up losing far more than you gain.

Once you have completed the interviews and follow-up questions, review the results. First, do the potential rewards of legal action justify the expense? Could those resources be used elsewhere with greater impact? Second, if the projected results justify the expense, which attorney impressed you the most? Would it make sense to hire several attorneys and have each handle a different aspect of the legal strategy?

Search among your supporters for an attorney willing to donate time to your cause. But, apply the same interview and selection procedures to "free" attorneys. A free attorney pursuing a faulty legal strategy is a liability, not an asset. Again, the bottom line in selecting an attorney is competence, not price.

Perhaps a volunteer attorney can help defray legal costs by conducting research for the hired gun. You should also explore opportunities to use other volunteers in doing legal legwork.

AFTER YOU HIRE AN ATTORNEY

Once you hire an attorney, make certain the two of you talk frequently. Ask for regular reports on the attorney's progress in executing the strategy that was outlined during the initial interview. If the attorney deviates from the strategy, ask for an explanation. If the attorney has difficulty justifying the deviation, you may have a problem.

While you should never substitute your opinion for the attorney's on legal matters, a competent lawyer should be able to justify his decisions with a plausible explanation. If the attorney gives vague answers or implies that you should simply trust him, you may have made a mistake. It is never too late to look for a better attorney.

The attorney must serve as an adviser to you and never attempt to impose his decisions upon you—you are the employer. The attorney should explain the facts, the options, and possible outcomes, then allow you to make the final choice about future action.

Resist the temptation to turn the whole campaign over to the attorney. While your lawyer advises you on the legal aspects of your campaign, you should pursue a parallel political strategy. As stated before, groups that pursue a sound legal strategy win about half the time. Groups pursuing a combined legal and political strategy win most of the time. But keep your attorney informed of actions pursued throughout your entire campaign.

Avoid using the attorney as your spokesperson. Except in a genuine legal proceeding, *you* should speak for your campaign. The attorney can never understand the issue as well as you do. After all, you live with the issue night and day. The attorney may have only begun thinking about the issue the night before a hearing. Therefore, you are in a better position to discuss the policies, wishes, and concerns of your constituents.

CHANGING THE LAW

What do you do when a proposed development will cause irrefutable damage but the law is powerless to act? One option is to change the law. Laws are made by the legislative branch of government, such as a county, city, or town council, the state legislature or general assembly, or Congress. Any member of the legislative branch or the chief executive officer (mayor, governor, etc.) can introduce a bill to change the law. If the measure receives a majority vote, it becomes law when signed by the chief executive.

In many areas, citizens have the right to petition government for a change in law. The process for using a petition is described in Chapter 7—Encouraging Decision Makers to Support Your Cause.

If a change in the law seems a viable way of achieving your goals, then do a little research. Talk to people who are familiar with the legislative body that will consider your proposal. Can you find a legislator to introduce your measure? How likely is success? How can you improve your chances of victory? People who may provide answers to these questions include: a friendly member of the legislative body, an attorney, the staff and officers of advocacy groups, and community activists who have worked with the legislative process in the past.

WHERE DO YOU GO FROM HERE?

Are you convinced that legal action will result in the attainment of your goals? If the answer is yes, the next step is to raise the funds needed to pursue legal action. Chapter 9—Mobilizing Support for Your Cause—describes how to research and test your options for raising money. The test results will reveal whether you have the potential to raise sufficient money to cover legal costs. If the potential is promising, make certain you launch a fund-raising drive early enough to have a retainer in hand by the date legal action must begin.

Go on to Chapter 7—Encouraging Decision Makers to Support Your Cause—to continue the process of formulating a political strategy.

7

Encouraging Decision Makers to Support Your Cause

DECISION MAKERS AND HOW DECISIONS ARE MADE

Decision makers are those people who are responsible for taking the actions essential to the attainment of your goals. No doubt you have identified a number of decision makers through the research suggested in the preceding chapters. The decision makers associated with most development issues will be:

- The property owner and his associates;
- Government officials; and
- Third parties, such as a land trust.

In the following pages, we will take a closer look at each of these decision makers and examine the factors they are likely to consider when asked to support your cause.

The Property Owner

Your ability to influence a property owner is usually a reflection of your power to affect the actions of other decision makers. For example, if a property owner wishes to retain his land in an undeveloped state but cannot afford the upkeep, the logical solution may be one of the preservation options described in Chapter 4.

It is unlikely that you can afford to preserve the land through your own resources. Instead, you must encourage others to take actions that will allow both you and the owner to attain your mutual goal of preserving the rural character of the tract. You may join forces with the owner to encourage acquisition by a parks agency or to find an easement option that will reduce property taxes to a level the owner can tolerate.

If your goals are in conflict with those of the property owner, the campaign becomes a contest to determine who has the greatest influence with other decision makers. Perhaps you and the owner will lobby local officials on a specific development constraint. You and your supporters will encourage the officials to impose the constraint in a manner consistent with your goals. The owner will lobby the officials to move in the opposing direction with the most likely outcome being a compromise.

If the property owner is committed to the development of his land, profit is a primary motivation. This is not meant as negative criticism. After all, our society is based upon profit, and it is just as important as any other human motivation. Nevertheless, your primary means of influencing an owner committed to development is through your ability to affect profit. If the owner perceives that it costs more to fight you than to compromise, he will start making offers.

The profit margin of a development venture is a product of far more than simply the ability to build houses as cheaply as possible and sell them for the highest price. Most development companies take care to build responsibly. A reputation as a "bad builder"—one who constantly cuts corners, ignores regulations, and treats public safety with a cavalier attitude—becomes a liability in the long run.

Bad builders find their proposals scrutinized more closely by regulatory agencies. Inspectors tend to hit the bad builder's site more frequently. The bad builder spends more time in court and may find insurance companies and banks avoiding his projects.

In summary, once an owner decides to develop his land, his willingness to negotiate with you will increase if resistance on the owner's part creates a public impression of intransigence.

The owner's desire to satisfy your concerns increases as:

• Your ability to influence the imposition of development constraints increases; and

• Your ability to invoke a public perception of the harmful aspects of the development grows.

Each added development constraint reduces the profitability of the venture. The immorality of a development is a function of the harm done to those affected by the project and the degree to which the developer is perceived as a greedy person. The willingness of other decision makers to support the development proposal declines as the immorality perceived by the public increases.

So by increasing public awareness of the damages associated with the project and by reducing profitability through development constraints, you should increase the property owner's willingness to negotiate with you. The more you can make both factors work in your favor, the more influence you will have with the owner.

Government Officials

The primary role of government in society is to provide for the overall public good, to protect people from threats to their health and safety, and to provide services essential to society, such as education, roads, pollution control facilities, and an endless list of other support functions.

Government also serves as a mediating body. Human values, needs, and desires vary over a broad spectrum. When one interest group clashes with another, it is frequently government's unpleasant task to resolve the dispute. This is particularly true in terms of development. Public attitudes towards development can be a complex mass of conflicting desires. Society demands affordable, safe housing. Yet, how much safety is enough? How stringently can government regulate home safety before costs are no longer "affordable"? Society demands affordable, safe housing that does not cause environmental pollution. At what point does government regulation of pollution control cause an "unacceptable" increase in housing costs? The role of mediator is not an easy one.

The decisions made by government are based upon three factors: the technical aspects of solutions, the legality of each solution, and the political repercussions of imposing solutions.

A solution may be any action that prevents damage or provides a benefit. Examples of solutions include: a pollution control device, an easement, building a new school, limiting the number of homes that may be built on a site, and all the other ways of reducing the impact of development upon society. The technical aspects pertain to the nuts and bolts of a solution. How well does the solution work? What does it cost? Is it the most cost-effective solution? Can it be enforced? How much maintenance does it require?

A solution must be consistent with the laws government uses to protect public health, safety, and welfare. The property owner cannot voluntarily pursue a solution that violates a statute intended to prevent traffic fatalities or control the spread of disease. And government cannot force a property owner to act unless it has the legal authority to mandate action. Should government attempt to extend its authority to the limits of the law, then the property owner may seek to block the move through the courts.

A government official must consider how interest groups and the general public will react to a given solution. Generally, the politically right thing to do is that which will enhance the official's image in the eyes of his supporters. For example, an elected official will resist an act that would cause voters to think unkindly of him, and a department head will not wish to make a decision vehemently opposed by his boss.

The key to winning the support of government officials is to find a way of achieving your goals through solutions that they find technically sound, legally defensible, and politically prudent. There are three levels of decision makers within government: elected officials, appointed officials, and staff. Each level of government may place a different emphasis on the technical, legal, and political aspects of decision making.

Elected Officials. Elected officials want to continue their political careers, and many aspire to a higher office. To fulfill this desire, they must win the confidence of a majority of the voters. Therefore, they fear situations that will cast them in an unfavorable light before their constituents. The more voters you sway to your side, the more influence you gain with an elected official. The key question is: Can you convince the elected official that a "significant" number of voters support your position?

The best way to learn how to prompt an elected official to act is to talk to people who have attempted to influence the decision maker in the past. Start asking questions around your area. Which citizen activists have attempted to influence the official? What did and did not work for them? At what point did the official decide to support the activist?

Talk to any of your supporters who are active in politics, particularly those who belong to the official's political party. The best source of information may be another elected official or someone who has managed a campaign for elective office.

Try to find out what is the official's base of political power. Did he get into office through the help of large contributions from the development industry or from those who benefit from building activity? If the answer is yes, your ability to influence the elected official may be poor.

How did the official do in the last election? Who were his constituents? Which voters supported the official? Perhaps the official won in a few key election precincts. If so, perhaps you can focus your efforts in these same areas and influence the official by demonstrating widespread support for your issue among the voters who put him in office.

Elected officials tend to be most concerned about the political aspects of an issue. Technical considerations must be overwhelming in order to counter the political benefits of a position. So, if you can demonstrate that he will gain supporters, you can probably influence an elected official to act on your behalf. This assumes, of course, that your position is sound both technically and legally.

Appointed Officials. Appointed officials serve at the pleasure of the chief executive officer, the mayor, county executive, governor, or the President. They are not elected to office. Normally the director or secretary of government departments or agencies are appointed. While the chief executive may hire and fire an appointed official, the legislative branch must approve (confirm) the appointment as well. Therefore, while an appointed official's primary motivation is to please the chief executive, he must also be responsive to the legislative branch.

Occasionally, appointed officials will serve as a shield for the chief executive. When a controversy is brewing, the executive will strive to focus attention upon the appointed secretary or director, saying that the decision rests with him.

By acting as a shield, the appointed official appears to be the bad guy, while the executive remains conveniently out of the picture. In this situation, it is in your best interest to refocus attention upon the chief executive. After all, the appointed official works for the executive. The executive always has the power to overrule an appointed official when a dispute arises.

But the executive will have difficulty overruling a subordinate if the appointed official has legitimate reasons for not acting. If you feel the appointed official's reasons are not valid, you must develop a way to refute his explanation for not supporting you. Only by developing a counterargument can you force the executive to step from behind the shield afforded by his appointed official.

Appointed officials tend to give equal weight to the technical and the political aspects of a decision. They will avoid a decision that will cost their boss supporters unless the technical considerations are over-whelming. You can probably win the support of an appointed official if you can satisfy his technical concerns, while demonstrating sub-stantial public support for your position. At a minimum, you must demonstrate that taking your side will not cost the appointed official's boss significant political support.

Staff. The vast majority of government officials occupy a staff posi-tion. They are normally protected by a merit or civil service system. It is difficult to fire an employee occupying a position protected through either system. While elected and appointed officials may change with each election, staff positions normally become vacant only when someone is promoted, leaves for work elsewhere, or retires.

The merit and civil service systems were established to end the practice of political patronage. In the bad old days, many government employees lost their jobs every time a new political party came into power. You either switched parties or found work elsewhere. Patron-age made for very poor government. The merit and civil service sys-tems provide the continuity and stability crucial to good public service.

People at the staff level tend to focus on technical considerations. Political questions are left to the appointed and elected officials.

For the most part, staff provide the technical expertise for govern-ment decision making. Much of the day-to-day work associated with government is left in the hands of staff. Appointed officials are pri-marily responsible for setting broad policy. It is up to staff to interpret and carry out the policies established by higher officials.

Frequently, your efforts to influence government decision making will begin at the staff level. If staff does not support your position, ap-pointed and elected officials will have a good reason (good from their perspective) for failing to act as you wish. Your chances of success will improve considerably if you can find a staff person who supports your position.

If you identify several solutions for a development issue, talk with the staff members responsible for implementing each solution. The best solution will be one that is supported by staff and has the greatest potential for satisfying your concerns.

CHOOSING POLITICAL ACTION TACTICS

The tactics described in the following pages are designed primarily to demonstrate increasing levels of public support for your position. Therefore, these tactics are most effective when your proposed solution is sound from both a technical and legal perspective, and the decision maker's refusal to support your cause is grounded in political concerns.

Avoid Making Enemies

When trying to decide which tactic to use first, always start with the softest approach. Always assume that decision makers wish to do the right thing. If they oppose you, assume it is because of a lack of understanding on their part, not because they are bad human beings.

It can be a tragic mistake to make an enemy out of someone who might have become an ally. Enemies tend to put logic aside and may continue to oppose you even when it no longer makes sense.

If a decision maker opposes your position or has not taken a position, foster the following attitude among your supporters: "We know that the decision maker wants to do the right thing, but he needs our support." So, instead of encouraging letters and calls that attack the decision maker, the message will be that of positive support: "We, your constituents, pledge our support if you go out on a limb and take the position we advocate in this cause." Such an attitude will greatly improve your potential for the winning decision-maker's support.

Winning Over and Keeping Decision Makers on Your Side

Your first contact with a decision maker should be through a tactic designed to determine his position on the issue and, if he is neutral or opposed, to learn why. Two of the tactics listed below are well suited for this purpose: the accountability session and lobbying.

After you have spoken to each decision maker, assign each to one of the following categories: supporting, undecided, and opposing. Future tactics should be selected to:

1. Keep supporting decision makers on your side.
2. Swing undecided decision makers to your side.
3. Detect any change in the thinking of opposing decision makers.

You should talk to each supporting decision maker frequently to ensure that they have not wavered. Lobbying is the best tactic to use in keeping the decision maker in the fold, particularly if the lobbyist is a solid supporter of your position and has a good relationship with the decision maker.

Unless an opposing decision maker is crucial to success, you should avoid using limited resources to turn him around. But, it is a good idea to periodically check with the opponent to learn of any change in his thinking. It is conceivable that your efforts to win over an undecided person may have caught the attention of the opponent. Perhaps he now sees that the political benefits of supporting your issue outweigh his reasons for opposing you.

Most of your resources should be focused upon undecided decision makers. Lobbying or accountability sessions can be used as a forum for responding to any technical concerns the decision maker voiced during the initial discussion. If you have made an honest effort to address the technical concerns and you feel the decision maker has the authority to act, yet the decision maker remains undecided, then escalate to one of the following political tactics: letters, petitions, or phone calls.

Each political tactic should be carried out, initially, by those people who have the greatest influence upon the decision maker. For example, letters to a councilman should come from people who not only live in his district, but reside in areas that strongly supported the councilman in the last election.

Use lobbying to maintain contact with the decision maker to assess the effect of the tactic. If the first round of letters, calls, or signatures did not cause the decision maker to alter his position, do not give up. Instead, encourage even more people to lobby the decision maker. Simultaneously, look for other opportunities to demonstrate public support for your issue, such as doing a mass turnout at an upcoming hearing or holding your own rally. Use the suggestions in the section on publicity to generate television and newspaper coverage of your issue.

Tracking Your Progress

The trouble with political action is the frequent difficulty of tracking progress. You may have flooded a decision maker's office with hundreds of calls or letters and still he has not budged. Then, all of a sudden, he announces a change of heart and elects to support your cause.

While the uncertainty associated with political action may be unavoidable, there are several steps you can take to reduce it.

1. Keep the lines of communication open. Continue lobbying the decision maker to detect opportunities to switch to other tactics that may prove more effective.

2. Always try to provide the decision maker with a graceful way of changing his position. New information is frequently used to justify such a change. Perhaps the decision maker says, "If I had only known this three months ago, I would have supported your cause from the beginning." Or an expression of public support can cause an official to alter his position. The official might say, "After receiving numerous calls and letters, it is obvious that the taxpayers want this land preserved. Therefore, I am now prepared to support acquisition of the tract."

3. Never condemn or offend the decision maker. If a decision maker fails to support your position, do not call him a bad person. Instead, try to find some positive way of encouraging a change in his position. Never imply that the decision maker has been bought off by the development industry. Or that he cares more for economic growth than public safety or the environment.

By carefully choosing your tactics and following these three steps, the likelihood of winning the decision maker's support will greatly increase.

Finally, always say thank you. Publicly thank a decision maker every time he acts on your behalf. Let all your supporters know of the decision-maker's good work and make certain the decision maker is fully aware of the public pat on the back.

TACTICS FOR WINNING THE SUPPORT OF DECISION MAKERS

Following are a number of tactics that can be used to encourage decision makers to act on your behalf. Tactics are usually designed to create an opportunity to request action on the part of the decision maker. Before making the request, verify that the decision maker has the power to take the action you desire.

Tactics work most effectively when a decision maker is forced to state his position in the presence of people he views as powerful, such as those who represent large numbers of voters and individuals who control sources of campaign contributions. During the execution of the tactic, the decision maker should be asked to state his position unequivocally. If he has not taken a position, he should be asked to explain why.

Accountability Session

An accountability session is usually the first tactic used to sway a decision-maker's thinking. It can and should be used with any category of decision maker. The purpose of the accountability session is to learn where the decision maker stands on the issue and why. The forum is normally a meeting between you, the decision maker and his staff, and your supporters.

Set up the accountability session by sending a letter to the decision maker requesting an opportunity to meet. The letter should clearly state your concerns, any thoughts you have for resolving your concerns, and specific steps you would like the decision maker to take.

Place a call to the decision maker a few days after the letter is mailed. Ask if the decision maker is interested in meeting with you. Try to learn what position the decision maker is likely to take. If you find that he is either undecided or opposed to your efforts, try to find out why. If you can, develop arguments to counter his concerns.

If the decision maker says he does not wish to meet, or fails to respond, try to find out why. Refer to the suggestions offered below on choosing tactics to plan your next step.

During the meeting, one individual should have the role of spokesperson for your group. If you expect a complex discussion, have specific supporters respond to questions pertaining to their area of expertise. At least one of your supporters should have the responsibility of taking detailed notes of everything that is said during the session.

Several members of your contingent should be viewed as powerful by the decision maker. To decide who, among your supporters, might fit this description, consider the decision maker's source of power and his perspective on the issue. If he is a staff person with a technical orientation, perhaps a university professor would be appropriate. If the decision maker is an elected official, include supporters who represent a large number of people, such as the president of the largest citizen organization in the official's district, a leading business executive (especially if the executive made a significant campaign contribution), an elected official, or a clergyman (preferably from the decision-maker's church).

Try to keep the number of people in your contingent between four and eight. Let the decision maker know who will be accompanying you to the meeting, particularly those he may view as powerful. The presence of powerful supporters will improve your credibility and help to keep the decision maker honest should his recollection of the meeting differ from yours. But be certain that each of your people is 100 percent on your side. The last thing you need is one of your supporters switching sides during the session.

Before the meeting takes place, do a rehearsal of the accountability session. Have a couple of people play the role of the decision maker and his aide. The best person to play the role of decision maker is someone who has had experience in a similar situation.

During the session, the decision maker may offer a solution or compromise that seems attractive. Resist the temptation to make any decisions during the meeting, particularly if you feel pressured by the decision maker. In fact, prior to the start of the session, get everyone to agree to avoid making any decisions during the session. If you are asked to make a decision, say, "I'm sorry but that is not possible. We do not constitute the entire decision-making body for our group. Before a decision can be made, we must talk with others in our group." If appropriate, you can say that the decision-maker's proposal is certainly interesting and that you and your supporters will give it full consideration.

A primary goal of the accountability session is to learn where the decision maker stands. If the decision maker states that he cannot support your position, ask why. If the decision maker offers vague reasons for opposing you, press for a specific answer. Do not be wooed by a charismatic decision maker who dodges the question by trying to switch the discussion to another topic. Bring the conversation back to his specific reasons for not acting on your behalf.

If you disagree with the decision maker's stated reasons for opposing you, tactfully explain your perspective. If he seems open to your perspective and seems to give it full consideration, take heart—his position may still be flexible. If, on the other hand, he swiftly rejects any opinion contrary to his, he is probably committed to his position.

If the decision maker says he cannot support you, hopefully he will offer legitimate reasons for his position. Listen carefully to what the decision maker says. In fact, just to make certain that you fully understand his reasons, say; "Let me make certain I heard you correctly." Then repeat what he said.

What if the decision maker has good reasons for opposing you? This can happen. If the reasons are so good that a change in his position is inconceivable, you may need to modify your overall strategy. But if you feel you can address his concerns in a way that may allow him to support you, ask for an opportunity to look into his concerns and to continue the discussion at a later date.

If the decision maker says that he has not taken a position on your issue, ask why. Find out what information he feels he needs to make a judgment. Ask what might encourage him to support you. If you feel you can satisfy his concerns by providing missing information, ask for an opportunity to research the issue further and reconvene the session later.

Generally, it is a good idea to confirm the key points of the session in a letter. The letter should be written shortly after the session adjourns, while the conversation is still fresh in your mind. Be certain to include points of agreement, disagreement, and any commitments. Conclude the letter by asking if it corresponds to the decision maker's recollection of the conversation.

Confrontational Tactics

Remember those tactics used so successfully by the civil rights and antiwar movement in the 1960s? Well, many of these tactics were confrontational. Tactics such as picketing, marches, rallies, sit-ins, and die-ins are used to force decision makers to confront and act on an issue.

Confrontational tactics work best when more conventional means, such as letters and petitions, have been used without producing results. Also, confrontational tactics become more appropriate as the urgency and human impact of an issue increases.

Again, confrontational tactics are intended to force decision makers to acknowledge an issue and take appropriate action. The effectiveness of the tactic increases with its visibility. In other words, confrontational tactics are particularly effective when they draw the attention of a TV news team and newspaper editors. The section of this chapter on publicity offers suggestions for attracting media attention to your confrontational tactics.

Before you escalate to confrontational tactics, be certain that you can demonstrate that you really tried to gain satisfaction by "working within the system." In fact, provide the press with copies of all your letters and other documents that show your repeated appeals for action. Prior to launching into confrontational tactics, seek out advice from people experienced with these tactics. At present, groups concerned about hazardous wastes are making considerable use of confrontational tactics. You can locate hazardous waste advocates in your area by contacting the Citizens Clearinghouse for Hazardous Waste, in Arlington, Virginia. Two of the references listed in Appendix A offer guidance on confrontational tactics: *Rules for Radicals* and the *Midwest Academy Organizing Manual.*

Letters

A letter-writing campaign can be an effective way of influencing government officials, particularly those who serve in elected office, as well as any other decision maker sensitive to public opinion. A well-written letter demonstrates that the author took the time to think about his position and is genuinely concerned about the issue. To a government official, this translates into a voter who will remember how the official acted come the next election.

It does not matter whether the letter is handwritten or typed. The important thing is that the writer presents logical reasons for his position and he makes it clear what he expects the official to do. If you ask for individually written letters, develop a fact sheet to serve as a guide for others to use in drafting their correspondence. A final benefit of the individually written letter is that it begs a response from the decision maker. This can become a real nuisance if the number of letters received is sizeable. The added pressure can only help.

Less effective, but still valuable, are "form" letters. A number of groups have used "fill-in the blanks" preprinted postcards. The postcard contains a message advocating action on the part of the decision maker and a place for the "writer" to sign his name. While a form letter does have an impact upon decision makers, the impact will not be as great as an individually written letter. But the sheer number of form letters generated may counter this drawback.

It is rare that you can get more than a handful of folks to write a letter. It is far easier to get a large number of people to sign a form letter. The impact of the form letter can be further increased by developing a means to let each signer know how the decision maker acted on the issue. Try to find a tactful way of letting the decision maker know that you plan to get back to each signer after he takes a position. Avoid stating this as a threat. An angry decision maker is less likely to support you.

Regardless of the type of letter generated, have each mailed directly to you, not to the decision maker. This step will allow you to keep an accurate count of the letters generated. Additionally, you will have a means of determining which methods of generating letters work best. Finally, you will learn who your active supporters are.

People that are willing to sign a letter are likely to volunteer for other tasks or contribute dollars as well. Get the name, address, and phone number of everyone who sends a letter in. If you receive an impressive number of letters, you can make a media event (see the section on publicity) out of delivering them to the decision maker.

The opportunities to encourage people to generate letters are endless. You can use direct mail, telemarketing, or canvassing as a means of asking folks to write a letter. Instead of soliciting a donation, you request a letter. Generally, you should avoid asking for two things at once, so resist the temptation to go for a letter and a donation. Whenever you hold a meeting, pass out blank paper and ask each attendee to take five minutes to compose a letter. You can also ask people to sign a form letter in any setting you might use for collecting signatures on a petition.

A close relative of the letter is the telegram. A number of national organizations encourage their members to use telegrams to lobby Congress. In terms of impact, a telegram falls between a form letter and an individually generated letter. The author must go to the trouble of composing the telegram, calling it in, and paying for it. This requires almost as much effort as writing a letter. Therefore, it sends a stronger message to the decision maker than a form letter. Perhaps one of the points favoring a telegram is the novelty of it. Perhaps more people will respond to a call for telegrams simply because they have never sent one before.

Many of the generalizations made above concerning letters from individuals also applies to correspondance from organizations. If an organization is in the habit of generating a letter for every issue that comes along and each letter sounds the same, the decision maker may not take the organization's position very seriously. If, on the other hand, the group is more selective and carefully constructs the arguments presented in its letters, greater impact will result—particularly if the organization copies each letter and promises to let the members know how the decision maker responded.

Lobbying

In the traditional use of the term, lobbying refers to a wide variety of tactics employed to influence decision makers. But, for the moment, it will be defined as attempts to sway the thinking of a decision maker by asking people he respects to speak to him on your behalf. The "respected person" fits the description of "powerful people," offered above under the heading of "Accountability Session." In fact, lobbying is quite similar to an accountability session. But only two people are involved in the lobbying session: the decision maker and your supporter.

The goal of lobbying is to demonstrate to the decision maker that an ever-growing number of influential people agree with your position. Your esteemed supporters talk one-on-one with the decision maker and encourage him to soften his position. Your supporter need not bring the decision maker to the point of changing his position. By steadily increasing the pressure, the decision maker may begin to look for ways to support your cause without being subjected to the embarrassment of reversing a prior position.

Mass Turnout

It takes a genuine interest in an issue to bring people out to a hearing, a rally, or some other mass event. Packing a hearing room with your supporters shows a decision maker that a large number of people are committed to your cause. If the decision maker is an elected official, or works for one, he will likely conclude that many of the attendees will remember the issue come the next election.

A variety of techniques can be used to encourage people to attend a mass turnout. You should make full use of the media (see the section on publicity). Additionally, methods described in Chapter 8, such as telemarketing, direct mail, and canvassing, can be used to turn out a crowd.

If you have never done a mass turnout before, look around for someone experienced in this tactic. Some of the people who are likely to have the necessary experience are: a union organizer, someone who has managed a political campaign, and the staff of advocacy groups.

If you have difficulty locating an experienced adviser, there are a few common pitfalls to avoid. Make certain that enough people show up to pack the room or hall to overflowing. It is far better to have a medium crowd in a small room than the same crowd in a large hall. Packing folks into a room will make your numbers appear even greater. Always recruit at least twice the number of people you need to pack the hall. Usually only half will show.

Once you are assured of a good turnout for your side, get the TV stations and reporters to cover the event. Again, the section on publicity offers suggestions for gaining media coverage.

Use some gimmick, such as a button or a colorful tag to wear, to let everyone know who your supporters are, and have a few folks hold up signs.

If you do not control the forum, make certain, in advance, that at least the spokesperson for your group will have a chance to speak. If the people controlling the forum do not provide you with an opportunity to state your case, interrupt the proceedings and demand your right to be heard. If your right to speak is still denied, order all your supporters to leave in protest and hold a press conference outside.

Petition

A petition can run the gamut from an informal means of gathering the names of supporters to a legal document calling for a new law.

A petition is headed with a statement about the issue and ends with specific language detailing what the signers want to achieve. A petition is frequently targeted at a specific decision maker. Below the heading, space is provided to sign, then print a full name, address, and phone number. Always ask for a phone number. You may want to contact the petition signers in the future with a request for further action.

A petition provides a means of demonstrating the extent of public support for your issue, and it is relatively easy to get people to sign a petition. (In fact, a portion of those who sign a petition will not remember inscribing their names if asked a few days later.) If used for this single purpose—to demonstrate support—petitions are probably about as effective as form letters. But, by no means should the petition be regarded as worthless. It does have an impact upon decision makers who are sensitive to public opinion.

You can increase the impact of the petition by keeping signers informed about the issue, which will increase their overall interest in your effort and stimulate their willingness to become active supporters. For instance, you can mail a brief update on the issue to petition signers. Let them know where the issue stands, what their signature accomplished, which decision makers are for, against, and undecided on the issue, and what the signer can do to help even more. At some point in the future, you can ask the sensitized petition signers to continue supporting the cause by writing a letter, attending a mass turnout, making a phone call, or sending in a donation.

People have the right to petition their government to change laws they find unjust. This right goes by different names around the country: referendum, initiative, ballot issue, proposition, and so forth. When used for this purpose, the petition must meet specific legal requirements, and a minimum number of valid signatures must be obtained. If both requirements are met, the question is placed before the voters during the next general election.

If you use a petition to change the law, your first step must be to talk with a competent attorney. You do not want to be in the disastrous position of having gathered 10,000 worthless signatures. Please do not overlook this step: get good legal advice. But don't end your research here. Talk to others in your area who have attempted to change the law through the right of petition. Find out what resources are required to successfully complete such a tactic. Remember, you don't win once you get the minimum number of signatures. In fact, the next step is much more difficult—getting a majority of the voters to support you at the polls.

Phone Calls

A calling campaign can demonstrate a high level of commitment to the issue if the callers provide a rational case for supporting the issue. Additionally, a flood of calls can tie up the decision-maker's office, providing him with an additional incentive for finding a way of dealing with you.

Volunteers can make the call from either home or the office. Each should be provided with no more than an outline or fact sheet of points to cover during the conversation. The call will be more effective if the volunteer uses his own words, rather than reading from a script.

When recruiting volunteers for a calling campaign, start with your most dedicated and articulate people. If anyone gets through to the decision maker, it will be the first few callers. Once the decision maker figures out what is going on, he will probably have an aide take all subsequent calls.

Publicity

Few tactics are quite as effective as newspaper and television coverage in gaining supporters and influencing decision makers.

It is unlikely that your mailings, phone calls, and other communications will reach as many people as a newspaper article or a TV news report. Also, media attention tends to bestow instant credibility on a campaign. When people read about your effort in the paper, it somehow becomes more real, more legitimate.

Elected officials and other decision makers know that voters base many of their decisions upon information gained through the media. A politician's chances for re-election improve each time a favorable article appears in the paper. A decision-maker's image declines every time a negative story runs on the evening news. If bad publicity continues, people will begin distancing themselves from the decision maker.

To gain exposure, you must offer something that is genuinely newsworthy; for example, a victory or a new development in your campaign. The value of a newsworthy item increases along with the significance of the item, particularly as it affects people.

Raising $10,000 is far more significant and newsworthy than raising $1,000. But the $1,000 may be significant for other reasons. Perhaps the money was raised in a unique way that makes it newsworthy. For example, receiving a $1,000 donation from a movie star is more newsworthy than $10,000 generated by telemarketing.

Making people, rather than things, the focus of your activities increases news value. Reporters will respond with more enthusiasm to a story of children playing in polluted water when compared to a tale of fish languishing in the same foulness. As the human element becomes more serious or tragic, the news value of the issue increases exponentially.

So what sorts of things make for a potentially newsworthy item in a land preservation or development campaign? Well, here are some possibilities: launching a dramatic new tactic; a highly successful fund-raising event; reaching a major agreement with a decision maker; uncovering a devastating impact; an impressive increase in the number of supporters; or discovering a factor that severely constrains site development.

Avoid the temptation to issue a press release on every new development in your campaign. Your group may acquire a reputation for generating non-news. Editors may develop the habit of trashing any envelope bearing the name of your organization.

Developing a good relationship with reporters and news editors will enhance the likelihood of gaining exposure for your issue. A good relationship is developed by providing news staff with press items that are genuinely newsworthy and based upon solid evidence. Equally important is the observance of deadlines. All forms of media must have adequate time to cover and report on news items. Preparing clear, concise press releases, public service announcements, and press packets will improve your relationship as well. If you consistently provide solid news items in an easy-to-use format, editors will be more prone to cover your issue.

In addition to the advice offered above, good follow-up on press releases and announcements will increase exposure. Call the editor or reporter a day or so after he should have received your mailing. Say you called to see if he had received the material and to answer any questions.

Poll your supporters to find someone who has experience with the press. Their guidance will bolster your publicity efforts. Many large corporations, institutions, and government agencies have public relations staff. If a school, business, or government official is supporting your cause, ask if their media relations staff might lend you a hand.

Media Events. A media event is staged for the primary purpose of generating publicity on an issue. The event must be sufficiently newsworthy to attract media coverage. It is generally a mistake to invite the press to a location if the only thing happening is someone talking. The exception, of course, is the announcement that is so startling, so urgent, that it cannot wait for the mail.

Public relations professionals have a simple rule-of-thumb for media events; don't do them. There are better ways of generating publicity that involve far less risk. What if you do a media event and the media fail to show because of a big fire on the other side of town? What if the media does show and they decide the event was not newsworthy?

Rather then staging an event for the sole purpose of gaining publicity, it is better to invite the press to cover activities done for some other reason.

Newspapers. A press release is the most common means of informing newspaper editors of newsworthy items. The release should summarize the who, what, where, when, and why of items you feel are worthy of publication.

Press releases should be double-spaced and kept to a maximum of two pages. The release can be placed on your letterhead with the word "NEWS" or "News Release" emblazoned across the top in bold letters. Place a statement near the top of the release that indicates who to contact for additional information. For example, "For further information, contact: John Jones, 801-333-3333."

Specify when the information contained in the release is available for publication. Most releases are cleared for publication as soon as they are mailed and carry the following language "FOR IMMEDIATE RELEASE." If, for some reason, you wish to postpone publication, use something like "RELEASE ONLY AFTER May 1, 1988." Better yet, time the mailing of the release so it will be received on the date of availability.

If your release pertains to an upcoming event, make certain it is mailed in advance of the newspaper's publication deadline. Most daily newspapers must receive a press release several days prior to your preferred publication date. Weekly or bi-weekly papers may require seven to 10 days to get your information into the correct edition. But please do not go by these guidelines alone. Call the newspaper, and find out when they need releases in order to run your material on a specific day.

When you issue a release for the primary purpose of getting people to attend an event, make certain that the information appears far enough in advance to allow people to schedule the event into their calendar.

Your release should be written to appeal to a newspaper editor or reporter. The release must impress the editor as being newsworthy. You must grab the editor's attention very early in the release. In fact, he will probably decide to run or reject your release after reading the title and first paragraph.

The title of the release must summarize the topic in a way that will spark the editor's interest. The title, like the entire release, should strive for a sense of urgency or the unusual, preferably both. The introductory paragraph should succinctly explain the who, what, where, when, and why, while continuing with the sense of urgency implied by the title.

Editors tend to use the material at the beginning of a press release and cut from the end. If your release is five paragraphs long and newspaper space is only available for three paragraphs, the editor will cut the last two. So, get a good distillation of your most important information in the first paragraph or two. Subsequent paragraphs should expand upon each point introduced at the beginning of the release.

Always include a phone number and an address to call for information in the body of the release. There may be folks who cannot attend your event, and the address/phone number will allow them to contact you with an offer of support.

Most newspapers have a section for running letters from readers. Usually the letters comment on a recent article that appeared in the paper. This section, called "Letters to the Editor," can provide a good forum for publicizing your issue. A surprising number of people read the letters to the editor. Also, newspapers have a history of printing many of the letters they receive.

Radio. Press releases should also be sent to the news staffs of radio stations. It may be helpful to modify the release into a "public service announcement"—or PSA,—particularly if it serves to notify people of an upcoming event. Radio stations generally prefer PSAs that will require a specific amount of time to read over the air, such as 10, 30, or 60 seconds. Give a few stations in your area a call, and talk to their news staff to learn their preferences.

Taped PSAs may serve as a way of gaining greater radio coverage. Before rushing out to buy blank tapes, talk to a local radio station to learn if they even accept prerecorded PSAs. If they do, ask what characteristics the tape must have. The station may even offer to develop prerecorded PSAs for you. Also, the media department at a local college may develop taped PSAs for your cause.

Television. Television defines "newsworthy" in a way that differs from the interpretation used by newspapers and radio stations. A story must have a strong visual component to attract the interest of television news editors.

You can get coverage for "talking heads"—someone speaking to a crowd—but it is not easy. The crowd must be large, or angry, and the issue must be highly controversial.

Television responds more readily to action stories where people are doing things other than talking. Examples include people marching, delivering petitions or sacks of letters to a decision maker, picketing, and other confrontational tactics.

A press release can be used to alert television news editors to an upcoming event. Try to get the release to the editor a week or two before the event. Television editors avoid committing news crews far in advance of an event. So call a day ahead of time to learn if the station will cover the event. If the station does plan to give you coverage, make a final phone call an hour before the event begins. The last call will let you confirm that the cameras will arrive. You will then have the option of delaying the climax of the event if the news crew is running late.

Other Sources of Publicity. Your press releases should be sent to magazines and newsletters that may have interest in your issue. Local magazines, as opposed to regional or national periodicals, are more prone to cover land preservation/development campaigns. Organizations supporting your cause may agree to publish your release in their newsletters. Magazines and newsletters range from weeklies to quarterlies with a deadline measured in days to weeks.

Fliers can provide a means of gaining quick, inexpensive publicity to a targeted group of people. A flier is usually printed on one side of a letter-size sheet. The topic of the flier is announced with bold lettering. The flier can be distributed like any other direct-mail piece, or you can use a "lit drop" to deliver the flier house-by-house. A lit drop can be done by car or on foot. When lit dropping by car, a passenger inserts a flier in newspaper boxes or attaches it to the outside of the mail box. Never put a flier inside of a mail box; it is illegal, and, without fail, one recipient of your flier will report you to the postmaster. When delivered on foot, fliers are left on doors or handed directly to residents. Generally, one volunteer can distribute 100 fliers per hour in a neighborhood of closely spaced homes. Fliers can be distributed at any location or event where people gather. But, before distributing fliers at a shopping center, church, business, or an event, get permission from the owner or manager.

Additional publicity can be gained through posters displayed at strategic locations. The poster should be large enough to contain essential information and be visible at a distance of 10 feet. Get the advice of an artist, an advertising specialist, or some similarly skilled person to help you develop an eye-catching design for your poster. At the very least, shop around until you find a printer who knows how to produce an effective poster.

TACTICS THAT MAY BE USED AGAINST YOU

Following is a description of some of the tactics that a decision maker may employ to counter your efforts.

Co-opting Your Supporters

A charismatic, powerful decision maker can be quite effective in converting people to his way of thinking. A private lunch in an expensive setting has caused more than one dedicated activist to question his own position. The decision maker will attempt to convince you that he's really a nice guy and intends to do the right thing, if only you will back off for a while and give him the time he needs to act.

How do you counter the charm? By insisting upon substance. If the decision maker is really a nice person, who wants to do the right thing, let him show his good faith by making a formal commitment. If he wants to negotiate, he must offer something more concrete than assurances.

Always wait 24 hours after meeting with a decision maker before acting on the results of the meeting. This will allow the charm to wear off. Ask yourself: What did I really get? Hopefully, if the answer is nothing, the decision maker got the same. If not, maybe you got taken.

Whenever one of your supporters has contact with a decision maker, a danger exists that he will be co-opted by the decision maker. The more contact with the decision maker, the greater the danger. If you have any doubts about a supporter, attempt to eliminate or minimize his contact with the decision maker. At a minimum, increase your contact with the supporter to reinforce his commitment to the cause.

Deflecting Criticism

As your tactics take effect, placing increasing pressure upon the decision maker, he may attempt to deflect your criticism somewhere else. He may propose a committee or task force to look into the issue further (also a great delaying tactic). Or he may insist that his hands are tied, and some other official must act first.

A decision maker may make a move that appears to be an attempt to deflect criticism, but it may also be a legitimate attempt on his part to resolve the issue. If he says he lacks the power to act, you must determine if this is true. If he does, in fact, lack the power to solve the issue, you should shift your tactics to a more appropriate decision maker. If the decision maker proposes a task force as a way of resolving the issue, you must decide if this is to your advantage. How will the task force improve the situation? What will you lose if you agree to the task force approach?

Delay

Delaying tactics serve to postpone the time when a decision must be made. If an uncooperative decision maker is lucky, he can delay the decision so long that everyone forgets about the issue. Calling for further research and study can be an effective delaying tactic. A period of weeks, months, or years may be required to complete the study. By the time the results are released, your supporters have long since lost interest, and much of your power has dissolved.

One of the most effective delaying tactics is to simply ignore you. The decision maker refuses to respond to your phone calls, letters, and your other attempts to discuss the issue. If you feel this tactic is being used against you, you should either:

• Move up the chain of command to find a more responsive decision maker;

• Attempt to communicate through someone the decision maker cannot ignore; or

• Pursue a solution that does not depend upon the decision maker.

If a decision maker makes a proposal that sounds like a delaying tactic, ask yourself: Will the proposed activity improve my chances of success? What will it materially contribute to the outcome of the issue? If the decision must be delayed, perhaps it is only fair to delay the development project as well.

Lawsuits

Can the decision maker, developer, or property owner sue you? Certainly he or she can, but it is quite unlikely. Generally, law suits are filed against citizens as an act of desperation and should be taken as a sign of a successful campaign.

Invariably, the suit benefits the citizen, not the decision maker. The publicity attendant to such law suits focuses a great deal of attention upon the issue. Public sentiment overwhelmingly goes to the citizen, while the decision maker bears the brunt of the public's wrath. With publicity and enhanced public support come additional dollars and volunteers. Few law suits ever reach court, and, if the citizen loses, the damages assessed are frequently small.

The exception to these generalizations about law suits is the situation in which the citizen fails to use common sense by doing things that are both unfair and damaging to the decision maker. Generally, a law suit will not succeed if you are raising legitimate questions about a land preservation or development issue. But, if you start printing newsletters that say the decision maker is a thief, cheats on his wife, and beats puppies, you may well get sued.

NIMBY

The term NIMBY stands for "Not In My Back Yard." It is applied to citizens as a way of portraying them as selfish people. If the tactic succeeds, others begin wondering if you really are being a selfish NIMBY.

NIMBYs do not want the development next to their home, but its okay if goes in someone else's backyard. NIMBYs force everyone to suffer so they can keep their little world just so. Because NIMBYs do not want the new industry in their backyard, the community is being robbed of jobs.

Labeling you as a NIMBY is an attempt at diverting attention away from the issue. To counter this tactic, create your own diversion to shift attention back to the key issues. Your countertactic should convey the following message: "We're not the people robbing the community of jobs. The decision maker wants to favor the development industry by ignoring the damages to the community. Now, to make things worse, by refusing to address the damages the decision maker is robbing the community of the jobs development might bring. Let's call for: YES to development and jobs; NO to development damages to the community!"

Outrageous Proposals

Occasionally, a property owner will propose a use for his land that raises hackles throughout the community. Even government doesn't like it. Sometimes the owner is serious, but he may simply be making a proposal knowing it will never fly, in hopes that he will be argued down to what he really wants.

For example, let's say that a tract of land is zoned for agriculture. The owner requests commercial zoning for the site so he can build a massive shopping mall. Everyone is aghast over the proposal as questions are asked like: How can you build a mall on that narrow, congested two-lane road? How in the world can the overloaded sewerline handle the thousands of gallons of sewage from all those shops and patrons? Won't a mall draw all the customers away from the existing shopping centers in the area?

So the community and government begin encouraging the owner to back off. He digs in his heels for a while and insists he has a right to commercial zoning. Then somebody gets the bright idea of offering to grant his zoning request if the owner agrees to a less disruptive commercial use. The owner then says, "Well, it just so happens that my land is ideally suited for a small office park." Government says Great, you've got it, and everyone breaths a collective sigh of relief, while the owner gloats to his friends how he got the zoning for his office park after all. And all his buddies in the development business said he was wasting his time.

How do you counter this tactic? Well, consider first whether it may be to your advantage to let the proposal ride. The truly outrageous proposal may also be a tremendous boon to your efforts to mobilize support. After all, the proposal is probably outrageous because it poses an unheard of threat to the community. A campaign to defeat the proposal may generate an overwhelming level of community support.

There are some things to look for that may help you to judge just how serious the owner's proposal is. For instance, if the owner has produced a detailed set of plans for the proposed use, he may be serious, particularly if he has invested a large sum of money. If the owner's property is unsuitable for the use and far better sites are available in the area, the proposal may be a deception. Finally, if the owner's proposal seems to be constantly changing, he's probably on a fishing expedition in search of a development venture that will just satisfy the community, while netting him the greatest return.

The "innocuous" proposal tends toward the opposite extreme. The owner seeks approval for some seemingly harmless use of his land. Once the approval is obtained, the owner is then free to pursue a hidden use that would not have been permitted if requested in a more open manner. This tactic provides one of those rare opportunities for killing a project after it has been approved. You will probably find government just as anxious as you to block the venture, unless, of course, the bureacracy was a knowing accomplice.

Secret Proceedings

People have a basic right to due process under the law. Those who may be adversely affected by an action have a right to be informed of the action beforehand, so they may ensure that their interests are protected. This philosophy is particularly applicable to government actions. A number of the permitting functions associated with the development review and approval process may have specific requirements for public notification. The developer may be required to post signs or publish a legal notice to announce the location and date of public hearings related to his project. When the developer or government fails to live up to public notification requirements, proceedings become secret.

If you find out about a proposed development when it is "too late" to influence decision making, find out what steps were taken to notify the public. Were public notification requirements met, as required by law, regulation, or policy? Get a copy of public notification requirements and review them for yourself. What documentation exists to prove that notification requirements were met, such as a clipping of a legal notice? If public notification requirements were not met, perhaps a good attorney can force the process to start all over again, giving you a fresh shot at protecting your interests.

Many government meetings are covered by "sunshine" laws. Sunshine laws require government to give public notice of upcoming meetings, hearings, and other proceedings so that any interested person may attend.

Splitting Your Base of Support

It is rare for a group of people to agree completely. This will also be true of your supporters. A skilled decision maker may attempt to divide your supporters, pitting the resulting factions against each other, while the development project marches on with only token resistance from your splintered campaign.

To illustrate how your group might be split, we will use a tract of land slated for intense residential development.

The only road leading to the site goes through an established community. If the tract is developed, traffic through the community will increase dramatically. The association representing the community fears the congestion and safety problems resulting from the increased traffic. On the proposed development site, there are ancient trees renowned for their magnificence and treasured by a local conservation group. The community association and the conservation group have joined forces to halt the development.

A skilled decision maker might attempt to neutralize the opposition to the development by making an offer one group cannot refuse, but can only accept by harming the other group.

The decision maker might approach the community association and say that he has found a way to solve the traffic concern. He can build a new road that will bypass the community completely. But, to construct the road along the alternate route, he must go right through the stand of ancient trees. He is willing to use the alternative route if the association will withdraw its opposition.

The decision maker might offer to create a tree sanctuary to protect the ancients, but only if the conservation group will drop its opposition to the development.

Both groups might be tempted to accept the decision-maker's offer. Before deciding, each must face some hard questions. What assurances exist to guarantee that the decision maker will live up to his side of the bargain? If they accept the decision-maker's offer and he backs out, can they stop the project without the other group? Is it right to accept the offer and abandon the other organization?

We Don't Believe Your Data

What if you come up with a study that shows that a proposed development will cause significant damage? Doesn't that guarantee victory for you? Not if the decision maker employs the tactic of questioning your data. Although it has many variations, the basic thrust of this tactic is to demonstrate that your study is not valid. The decision maker's actual reason for questioning the study may be to avoid being forced to support your position.

For example, study results will probably come from research done in an area other than where the site in question is located. The decision maker may claim that the study does not apply because conditions at the site are different from those where the study took place. If this argument is used, contact the person who conducted the study, and ask if the results seem applicable to your site. If the answer is yes, relay this information to the decision maker. If he still insists that the results are not applicable, yet fails to offer a logical basis for his belief, then he may be using a tactic on you. If you feel the acceptance of the study is crucial to your success, look for a more objective forum for settling the dispute. Try to place the issue before a higher decision maker or before the public.

Another variation of the same tactic questions the way in which the study was conducted. Rare is it that study methods are perfect and conclusions are irrefutable. In even the best of research, there is always a margin of error. A decision maker may argue that the study was done in such a sloppy manner that the results are highly suspect. Again, contact the author of the study and get his opinion. If you still believe the study is valid, ask how he would proceed if forced to defend his research.

If your data is called into question, give some careful thought to the situation. Ask yourself just how important is it that the data be accepted? How much is acceptance worth in terms of your time and resources? Do not allow the acceptance of your data to become an emotional issue for you. Take care if you find yourself thinking, "How dare they question my credibility by attacking my data. I'll show them!" It is easy to lose sight of your real goals when the ego becomes entwined in such a contest. Remember, attaining your goals is the important thing, not how they are attained.

If your data is questioned, try to analyze the decision-maker's motivations. Does he really question the data, or does he fear the position he will be in if forced to accept the data? It may be more productive to look for opportunities to help the decision maker comfortably deal with the position he fears, rather than spending all your effort defending your data.

WHERE DO YOU GO FROM HERE?

Now you know:

- Which decision makers have the power to take actions that will lead to the attainment of your goals?

- Of those decision makers, which you can influence to act on your behalf? and

- What tactics you can use to win the decision-maker's support?

It is now time to go on to Chapter 8, where you will assess the number of dollars, volunteers, and influential people available to your campaign. This assessment will allow you to determine which tactics you can successfully carry out. Each tactic will have a cost in terms of dollars and volunteers. Both are limited resources. As you acquire the necessary resources, you should launch both your political and legal campaign for attaining your goals.

8

Mobilizing
Public Support
for Your Cause

In this chapter, you will learn how to recruit the people who can make your campaign a success through their contributions of dollars, volunteer hours, and influence. But you will only win their support if you can demonstrate that:

- Your issue is an immediate threat to their interests;
- You have an effective strategy for averting the threat; and
- The strategy can only be successfully carried out with the active support of each person who benefits from your campaign.

The funds provided by your supporters may be used for mailings, posters, and other publicity tools, legal fees, expert witnesses, fundraising efforts, and tactics designed to sway decision makers. The hours contributed by your supporters may be spent while fund raising, conducting research, executing political actions, such as a letter-writing drive, or the dozens of other tasks essential to a successful outcome. Among your supporters you will find people who have the power to influence the actions of decision makers. Combined with large numbers of supporters, your influential allies will give your campaign the political clout essential to victory.

If your experience with mobilizing supporters is limited, look around for an adviser. Many advocacy groups spend a considerable amount of time raising funds, training and managing volunteers, and executing political action tactics. Advice on volunteer recruitment may also be obtained from hospitals, social services agencies, and a wide variety of services organizations such the Lions, Rotary, Jaycees, and the League of Women Voters. Other entities active in fund raising include colleges and universities, service organizations, and just about any other nonprofit group. So before you launch into a drive to mobilize supporters, seek the advice of the staff or officers of these groups.

IDENTIFYING POTENTIAL SUPPORTERS

Your supporters include everyone who may be affected by your issue. Actually, these folks will be "potential" supporters until you ask them for dollars, hours, or to use their influence on your behalf.

If you went through the goal-setting process described in Chapter 2, you are ready to begin identifying potential supporters. Think about the damage that might result from a development venture. Who would be concerned about the damage? If the project will cause overcrowding at a local school, the PTA may support your effort. Support may also come from all those with children attending the school as well as the teacher's union. A dramatic increase in traffic volume may bring support from all the folks living along major roads in the surrounding area.

Examine each of the benefits afforded by the tract in its current state. Who would be concerned about the loss of these benefits? If the area serves as unofficial parkland, all those who use the land are potential supporters. Finally, consider any benefits that might result from limited or partial development of the tract. If the goal of your campaign is to eliminate the damages while allowing the benefits of development to occur, each person who would reap these benefits may be a potential supporter.

Compile a list of all potential supporters. Identify those who are most likely to benefit from your campaign. If the list is long and your resources are limited, it makes sense to start soliciting support from those folks who are most likely to say yes. Obviously, those most apt to offer support are those who will benefit to the greatest degree from your efforts.

Find out if these people are organized. Is there a group that may count these folks as members? If so, your first contact should be made through the leadership of whatever group they belong to.

Generally, the leadership of each organization will know how their members will react to the issue. If the leadership supports your cause, usually their members will as well. The leadership can also help you to define the issue in a way that would generate maximum support from their members.

It is important to contact potential supporters early. If you include them in the decision-making process from the beginning, the depth of support they offer will increase as the campaign evolves. At the very least, you should contact the leadership of those groups representing potentially strong supporters. Tell the leaders what you are up to, the damages and benefits you have identified, and offer them an opportunity to help you decide how to deal with the issue.

A wide variety of skills may be required to launch a campaign to deal with a proposed development project. These skills may include: fund raising, community organizing, lobbying, publicity, management, accounting, legal advocacy, scientific research, land appraisal, and a host of other talents. People with these skills may be found among your supporters. And since they are your supporters, essential skills may be offered at a reduced cost or free of charge.

As new supporters join your cause, survey each to learn their concerns. Make certain that your campaign will resolve all of the concerns of your supporters, or at least those concerns shared by the majority. Additionally, find out if new supporters would be willing to donate time to the campaign. Provide each with a list of volunteer tasks associated with the effort. Ask which tasks they would care to help with, then follow through by swiftly scheduling an opportunity for the newcomer to pursue the task.

BASIC TECHNIQUES FOR MOBILIZING INDIVIDUAL SUPPORTERS

There are three basic techniques for recruiting individual supporters: direct mail, telemarketing, and canvassing. But before getting into these techniques, a few words will be offered about the importance of individual supporters to your campaign.

Individuals account for more than 80 percent of the charitable dollars given in this country. But, individual supporters provide far more than mere dollars. Each contributor may also be a voter. As your ranks of supporters expand, the political clout of your campaign will grow as well.

Elected officials will watch with increasing interest as your supporters grow in numbers. They will wonder: "How many of these people will remember how I acted on this issue come the next election?" "Will

I be perceived as being for the people or in the pocket of the building industry?"

A large base of individual supporters provides an equally large pool of volunteers. The volunteer pool can be called upon to pack hearings or jam the phone lines at city hall. Among your volunteers, you may find people willing to donate essential skills, such as accounting, legal advice, clerical services, or expert testimony.

Potential individual supporters, or prospects, are categorized as hot, warm, or cold. A hot list of prospects includes folks who have contributed to your cause within the past year. Prospects on a warm list are either lapsed members or active supporters of a similar cause. A cold list is composed of prospects who have never supported your cause, nor a similar one, but may be impacted by the issue and, therefore, will benefit from your campaign.

Canvassing

Through canvassing, a request for support is made face-to-face with the prospect. Most canvassing is performed by knocking on the prospect's door. Door-to-door canvassing works best where homes are close together, crime rates are low, and local law permits canvassing. A canvass can also be conducted on a beach, in a shopping center, an office building, or any other location where people gather.

Canvassing is the best technique to use when you need something in addition to a donation, such as a signature on a petition. Canvassing is most successful when carried out by well-trained volunteers who are just as threatened by the issue as the prospects. A well-managed canvass should yield a response rate exceeding 50 percent.

It is fairly easy to entice volunteers into a direct-mail campaign. The worst thing they are asked to do is stuff envelopes. Recruiting volunteers for calling is moderately difficult. After all, asking strangers for money can be a bit intimidating, even over the phone. But the most difficult task is recruiting people to canvass.

With both phoning and canvassing, volunteer training and management are exceedingly important. A good training program will do much to allay volunteer fears and increase the rate of success. If you decide to use canvassing, try to find someone experienced with this technique to help you.

Following is an approach you can use to launch a canvassing campaign. Have your volunteers go door-to-door asking for something that is both easy for people to do and will serve to test the prospect's interest in the issue. Many canvasses use a petition for this purpose. Once a prospect signs the petition, the canvasser then asks for a contribution, or a letter or a phone call, to a targeted decision maker.

Hold a training session for your volunteers before you send them out to canvass. Cover the same points for training telemarketing volunteers offered in Appendix B. Provide your volunteers with a script to review. Encourage your canvassers to modify the script so it fits their speaking style. Following is a sample canvassing script. Hello, Mr. Prospect. Hi, my name is Ms. Volunteer. I'm a volunteer with (*name of your group*). Have you heard about the big highway they are planning to put through our community? (WAIT FOR RESPONSE; if it is no, describe the threat.) The association has launched a campaign to stop the highway. Our first step is to gather 1,000 signatures on a petition protesting the highway. (HAND THE PETITION TO THE PROSPECT.) "Will you help us protect the community by signing the petition?" (IF THE PROSPECT SIGNS THE PETITION, THEN CONTINUE. OTHERWISE POLITELY END THE CONVERSATION.) We also hope to raise $5,000 to fund our campaign to stop the highway. Many of your neighbors, including me, have contributed. Can we count on you for a donation? (WAIT FOR RESPONSE; if yes, say you will gladly wait while the prospect gets a check.)

If you canvass from home-to-home, limit the hours to 6:00 PM to 9:00 PM, Monday through Thursday. It is also a good idea to have canvassers work in teams of two for both moral support and safety. You can have one canvasser work one side of a street while her partner knocks on doors along the other side of the street.

Direct Mail

A letter is sent to a list of prospects. The letter states the need, describes how the need impacts the prospect, describes your solution, and asks for the prospect's support so you can implement the solution. If the desired action is a donation, a return envelope should be included in the mailing to ease the prospect's task of sending you a check. A brochure or other materials describing your cause may also be included.

At first glance, direct mail appears to be a great way to generate support. The cost seems small, and volunteers are not compelled to ask for support directly. Sadly, the rate of return on direct mail frequently negates the advantages. With a cold list of prospects, you can expect a response rate of 0.5 to two percent. For every 1,000 pieces you mail, five to 20 people will support your cause. When used as a fund-raising technique, you are lucky to recover your costs on a mailing to a cold list. On a warm and hot list, the respective rates of return range from two to five percent and 10 to 60 percent.

Direct mail does have the advantage of being relatively easy to test. You make a mailing to a small sample from each prospect category (hot, warm, and cold) and see if the returns are worth the effort. A sample direct-mail letter is included on the following page. References on direct mail will be found in Appendix A, under the heading of "Fund Raising."

Generally, direct mail is best suited for generating support among warm and hot prospects, particularly if telemarketing is used to follow up on those who failed to respond to the mailing.

Telemarketing

As the name implies, phone calls are made to prospects. Calls are made in the evening from a location with a number of outgoing telephone lines. Initially, volunteers attend a half-hour training session during which they have a chance to deal with their fears and to learn effective telemarketing techniques. A well-managed telemarketing campaign can raise $100 to $200 for each hour of volunteer phoning, with costs coming in at less than 20 percent of the gross proceeds. The response rate on cold and warm lists ranges from 20 to 60 percent. This method is particularly effective if calls are made by volunteers who, like the prospect, are threatened by the issue. Telemarketing has proven to be a particularly effective method of mobilizing support for a campaign to deal with land development issues. Therefore, a detailed description of telemarketing is provided in Appendix B.

FUND RAISING

Although it is possible to win without money, success is far more likely with an ample treasury. Money may be needed for legal fees, land acquisition, research, mailings, advertisements, and a hundred other items. Also, nothing is quite as effective in demonstrating widespread support for your issue as a large number of donors.

Fund raising is not begging. Your values are just as important as the next person's. You view land development as a potential threat to things you value. No doubt others share your values and will also perceive development as a threat. Fund raising at its best consists of:

research to identify those who may share your concerns, informing them of the impending threat, and offering them an opportunity to join with you in averting the danger. So fund raising is not begging, it's helping others to combine their resources with yours to protect shared values.

SAMPLE DIRECT-MAIL
FUND-RAISING REQUEST

Forest Hills Community Association, Inc.
P.O. Box 333
Forest, MD 33333

January 2, 1990

Dear Neighbor:

Future development in the Forest Hills area may consume 10,000 acres of land! The Forest Hills Association has launched a campaign to protect your home and neighborhood from the damages resulting from poorly planned development. I would like to offer you an opportunity to join with me and many of our neighbors in making this campaign a success.

Those of us who serve on the board of the Forest Hills Association do not believe that development is inherently bad. In fact, growth can be beneficial. We do object to past poorly planned development that has brought congested intersections to our area, along with well and septic system failures, polluted streams, and the loss of scenic landscapes.

There could be 4,000 housing units built on the 10,000 acres of land zoned for development in our area. Each housing unit will generate 10 car trips per day. That means 40,000 more car trips on the roads serving your neighborhood and mine. Each new home will daily draw 350 gallons of water from the ground, through a well, then release an equal amount of wastewater back into the ground by way of a septic system. The amount of wellwater and sewage cycled through these 4,000 housing units comes to a staggering 1,400,000 gallons per day!

Through our campaign, we will work to ensure that development only occurs when it can be demonstrated that:
 • The added use of groundwater will not cause existing wells to run dry;

- The release of more sewage into the earth will not pollute wells and streams;
  - Roads can safely handle the additional traffic;
  - The proposed housing units will not unreasonably detract from the rural beauty of our area; and
  - Police and fire services can fully protect both existing and new residents of the area.

The Forest Hills Association is an effective means of ensuring well-planned growth. We recently won 34 separate battles to maintain low-density zoning on 517 acres of rural land in our area! As impressive as our past victories have been, we know they are not enough. If we are to succeed in protecting our community from the development of nearly 16 square miles of land, we must launch a far more ambitious campaign.

The projected budget for the campaign crucial to our future welfare is $25,000. These funds will be used for land preservation activities, legal defense, public education, and evaluating proposed development projects to determine if existing homes will be harmed. We urgently need your support so we can build upon our past successes and protect your home and ours.

Please use the accompanying, self-addressed envelope to make your donation today.

Yours for a Safe Community,

John Smith, President
333-333-3333

Funds may come from a variety of sources—individuals, foundations, government, and a number of other providers. Research is an extremely important step in fund raising, as well as all other aspects of a campaign. Good research can allow you to focus your time and resources on those funders most likely to support your cause.

All fund-raising appeals, regardless of who the appeal is directed to, must follow a basic pattern. This pattern consists of three essential elements: 1) a description of a threat that directly impacts the prospect; 2) a credible strategy that will avert the threat; and 3) a clear statement demonstrating that the prospect's help is crucial to implementing the strategy (in fact, without the prospect's support, the strategy cannot be implemented). If the appeal can be transmitted with a sense of urgency, by someone acquainted with the prospect, the level of support will be even greater.

Once prospects have been identified and an appeal has been drafted, a test should be conducted. A test is performed by exposing a portion of your prospects to the appeal. The results will allow you to determine how well you have done in researching and identifying prospects. The results will also demonstrate the effectiveness of the appeal for support. Testing provides an opportunity to find the best supporters among several groupings of prospects, or to try several different appeals among a specific category of prospects. Ultimately, testing provides a way of learning how much support may be available to your cause.

An Initial Budget

The expenses associated with most campaigns fall into three categories: political action, litigation, and land acquisition. Political action includes the work done to find and recruit supporters and to encourage decision makers to act on your behalf. The costs associated with litigation result from legal research, the use of attorneys for negotiations, and court action. Land acquisition is self-explanatory. The costs associated with each category of activity fall into the following ranges:

Political Action	$100–$2,000
Litigation	$5,000–$40,000
Land Acquisition	$100,000–$ millions

Sources of Funding

Funds may be obtained from: government, foundations, land trusts, corporations, citizen organizations, and individuals. Following are some generalizations about each funding source and the activities they may support.

1. Government, foundations, and land trusts are the most likely source of the large sums needed to acquire land.

2. Most government agencies, foundations, and land trusts will avoid underwriting litigation costs. Typically, legal defense funds are built through contributions from individuals, citizen organizations, and, occasionally, corporations.

3. Funds for political action usually come from individuals and citizen organizations.

Land trusts were discussed in Chapter 4—How to Preserve Land. Another source of funds that will not be addressed below are individuals who contribute less than $100. Generally, these small contributions make up less than 30 percent of the total amount received by a campaign. But, while small donations may not be a major source of income, this category must not be ignored. Yes, small contributions may account for less than a third of the income, but the people who make these donations may constitute 75 percent of your total number of supporters. Therefore, the real importance of this funding source is the potential for volunteer hours, influence, and political clout a massive number of supporters can offer.

The most effective techniques for soliciting donations under $100 are: canvassing, followed by telemarketing, then direct mail. The more your campaign relies upon political action, as opposed to litigation, the more aggressively you should pursue supporters who may contribute an average of $20. In the final analysis, the political power represented by masses of individual donors may contribute more to your victory than the best lawyers money can buy.

Citizen Organizations. Citizen groups that may support your campaign include: local improvement and neighborhood associations, community councils, sportsmen clubs, environmental and conservation groups, watershed associations, and historical societies. These organizations can contribute to your fund-raising effort in three very important ways. First, the officers of the group may offer a donation out of their treasury. Second, the organization may allow you to use their membership list to solicit further support. Third, they can offer advice on fund raising, particularly on techniques that work best among their own members. Suggestions were offered in Chapter 5—Resolving Specific Development Issues—for locating advocacy groups. These same suggestions can be used to identify other citizen organizations that may support your cause.

Corporations. Think about the corporations in your area. Are there any that might benefit from your campaign? If your effort succeeds, would a specific corporation or industry benefit either through the elimination of a potential competitor or increased sales? Do you or any of your supporters have a friend in the upper echelons of a corporation? If you answer yes to any of these questions, you may succeed in winning corporate support for your cause.

Begin by asking questions about each candidate corporation. Try to learn the patterns of charitable giving within the corporation. These patterns will provide an indication of whether the corporation supports causes such as yours.

Look for people who have been particularly successful in winning corporate support, such as professional fund raisers, the staff of nonprofit groups, or church administrators. If you find someone who is both experienced and cooperative, ask for their help in tapping into corporations for support.

Contact each corporation you have targeted for a funding request. Ask to speak to the executive who handles requests for financial support. Describe your campaign and how it may benefit the corporation. Inquire about the potential for gaining support from the corporation. If the potential is good, ask for an opportunity to meet with the executive to discuss the request at greater length.

Foundations. Foundations are nonprofit organizations established to provide support for charitable causes. Foundations disperse money through grants made to individuals, organizations, or institutions. Despite the fact that foundations account for only five percent of the charitable dollars given in the U.S., foundations tend to be the first place people look to for funding. Before joining the rush for foundation money, consider the fact that foundations receive more grant applications than they can ever approve. Also, several months to a year may elapse before a decision is made on your application. Finally, many foundations invest a portion of their assets in real estate. Therefore, few foundations may be willing to support your campaign if the goal is to restrict development.

A national organization known as "The Foundation Center" has established at least one location in each state where references on foundations can be viewed. You will find the address and phone number of The Foundation Center listed in Appendix A, under "Fund Raising."

In each center, you will find the *Foundation Directory.* This book lists all the foundations that have made grants within each state. By looking through the directory, you can locate foundations that have made grants to causes resembling yours. If none are found, look at each foundation's giving criteria. If your cause does not meet any of the criteria listed in the directory, your chances of winning a foundation grant are poor, at best.

If you identify a foundation that may support your cause, contact their executive director or president. Arrange to meet with the foundation official to learn what your chances are of winning a grant. If the prospects look good, ask how you should proceed in submitting an application for financial support. Excellent references on grant writing are available through The Foundation Center. Also, several grant-writing guides are listed under "Fund-Raising," in Appendix A.

Government. The chapter on land preservation described how to research the potential for securing acquisition funds through government agencies. Although it is quite rare for government to underwrite legal costs, other options may be available. For instance, if you convince government to refuse an essential permit for a proposed development, government attorneys must defend the decision, not yours. Some local and state governments have a people's counsel to provide legal services for qualifying citizens and organizations. But, before totally dismissing government support for your efforts, talk with a local advocacy group. Tax dollars are available for some issues. For example, government funds may be provided to groups wishing to hire their own experts to examine hazardous waste issues.

Major Donors. A major donor is anyone who contributes a $100 or more. A campaign to recruit major donors consists of the following steps:

1. You and your active supporters identify people meeting the following criteria: the prospect has the ability to make a donation of $100 or more, the prospect will benefit from the campaign, and the prospect is acquainted with someone active in the campaign.

2. Each acquaintance is asked to write a letter to the prospect. The letter explains the issue, the campaign's strategy to deal with the issue, how a successful outcome will benefit the prospect, describes the financial need, and ends with a request for a meeting.

3. The acquaintance calls the prospect and sets a date to meet.

4. During the meeting, the points addressed in the letter are covered again, and a request is made for a specific amount, usually $1,000 or more. By starting the request at a high figure, like $1,000, the size of the average donation is increased considerably.

A major donor campaign is frequently used to launch a large fund-raising effort. Prospects are told that their sizeable donation will serve to inspire others to contribute. And, indeed, major donors account for much of the income of established groups. In fact, 85 percent of the income received by many groups comes from the top 30 percent of their supporters—folks who gave $100 or more.

Consult the references listed in Appendix A prior to launching a major donor campaign. Armed with the information gained from these references, go through the four steps described above. Initially, test the campaign with a few prospects. You will learn a lot from the experience. But, if the results are disappointing, do not give up on major donors. Instead, try to find someone with experience in this fund-raising activity. Ask the experienced person to analyze your results and determine if it's worth another try.

Frequently, major donors can provide you with an inside track on winning support from foundations, corporations, land trusts, and government.

Sales and Events. This category of fund raising includes raffles, yard sales, selling merchandise such as T-shirts, and selling space in an ad book. Generally, sales are not the most effective way to fund a campaign. A significant portion of the income may go to paying for merchandise, awarding a prize, or other costs. This diminishes the amount remaining for the campaign and increases your "up-front" costs. Additionally, other fund-raising techniques, such as direct mail, telemarketing, and canvassing, are more effective in focusing the attention of the prospect on the issue. Sales tend to emphasize the benefits of buying the item rather than supporting the cause. But, if the cause is weak, sales may be the right fund-raising activity.

Dances, bull roasts, and concerts are typical fund-raising events. The intent is to offer something of value along with an opportunity to support a cause. Like sales, an event may be expensive to put on with the attendant danger of taking a loss. But events and sales make it possible to greatly expand the potential number of supporters. Perhaps the proper role for both fund-raising activities is that of an adjunct to more direct means of generating money. In other words, if telemarketing or canvassing fails to raise sufficient funds, you should consider a sale or event. Both can be a good way to add to your mailing list names of people who can then be "converted to your cause" through a newsletter or other educational techniques. Perhaps the best reference on sales and events is *The Grass Roots Fund-Raising Book* (see Appendix A).

A BASIC FUND-RAISING STRATEGY

Begin your fund-raising drive among the members of your core group. The core group is made up of those three to 30 people who feel directly threatened by a development venture. These are the folks who come to most of your meetings and do the majority of the work.

During the research stage of a campaign, financial needs can usually be counted in the tens of dollars. For the most part, these minimal expenses are covered by each core-group member as they happen to incur an expense. Costs escalate dramatically once legal or political action is contemplated.

When your campaign reaches the point of hiring a lawyer or mobilizing supporters for letter writing or phone calls, you should launch your fund-raising effort. Gather all of your core-group members together and explain the campaign strategy. Allow the core group to ask questions and propose changes to the strategy. Once you reach consensus, present the projected cost to carry out the strategy. Provide the core group with an opportunity to examine your cost estimates. When they feel comfortable with the accuracy of your estimates, ask each member of the core group to make a contribution towards the costs to carry out the strategy.

Each core-group member should be asked to make a contribution that is significant for them. Generally, the amount should fall somewhere between two to five percent of each member's average annual income. You can give everyone an idea of how much they should consider by being the first to write a check. Your contribution should be at the upper end of the two to five percent of annual income range. Make certain everyone knows how much you contributed. Announce the figure while standing before the core group as you make out your check.

Another way of suggesting an amount would be to ask each core-group member to consider how the development venture may affect the value of their property. Ask each member to consider making a contribution equal to 10 to 50 percent of the loss in property value should the proposed venture become a reality. Point out that even a donation equal to 50 percent of the loss of value is still a bargain. After all, isn't it better to pay half as much to keep the development from happening than to lose twice that amount through a decline in property value?

If the contributions from the core group fail to produce sufficient funds to carry out your strategy, pose two options to the core group: each member could dig a bit deeper and/or core-group members can participate in an expanded fund-raising effort.

The first step in an expanded fund drive should be a major donor solicitation. Review your list of potential supporters for major donor candidates. Ask each core-group member to identify at least one person they know to solicit for a donation of $100 or more. Generally, a request for $500 or more should be made using the one-on-one meeting approach described above under the heading of "Major Donors."

Solicitations for $100 to $500 can be handled in a less personalized manner. Each core-group member should invite the potential midrange donor to a coffee, tea, or wine and cheese party. The invitation should be extended through a phone call or a hand-written note. The evening of the event might unfold as follows. Allow everyone to socialize and munch on hors d'oeuvres for 15 minutes or so. Then ask the prospects to take a seat and begin your presentation. Describe the issue, explain how it will directly affect each person, and present your strategy for averting the threat. Allow half an hour for questions. Then present the cost to carry out the strategy. Describe the results of your fund-raising efforts thus far. Make it clear that all the core-group members have donated substantially, but it still is not enough. Drive home the point that the strategy will only succeed if you can reach your fund-raising goal. And without the support of each prospect, you cannot raise sufficient funds to protect all those who are present. End the discussion with a clearly stated request for a specific amount. Then pull out your own checkbook again and write out a check equal to the maximum amount you suggested to those present. Have pledge cards available for anyone who did not bring their checkbook. The card need have nothing more than space for a name, address, phone number, and pledge amount. You can also provide each person with a stamped, self-addressed no. 6 envelope for mailing in their check.

Once you have exhausted the potential major and midrange donors, expand the fund-raising effort through less personalized solicitations, such as telemarketing or canvassing. Ask each new donor if they know of any prospects for a major or midrange donation. Set up one-on-one solicitations or an additional coffee as new candidates for large contributions become available.

SEARCHING FOR INFLUENCE
AMONG YOUR SUPPORTERS

The purpose of this search is to locate people who support your cause and who can help you to convince decision makers to act on your behalf.

A supporter may be influential because he is a friend of a decision maker or a respected member of the community. Respect may be due to the position your supporter holds in the community or the fact that he has the ability to give the decision maker something he wants.

Some examples of people who may be respected by a decision maker because of position are: members of the Chamber of Commerce; the dean or chairman of a college or university department; a clergyman from a powerful church; the chief executive officer of a major corporation; a newspaper editor; or the president of a large citizens organization. Examples of people who can grant something desired by a decision maker include: a wealthy person (a campaign contribution), a celebrity (prestige or an endorsement), or a corporate executive (a future job).

There are several ways to find these influential people among your supporters.

Frequently, major and midrange donors meet the definition of an influential person. If the prospect is willing to contribute money to your effort, he will probably lend his influence as well. As you explain your campaign strategy to the prospect, mention the names of the decision makers you plan to approach. Ask the major donor if he knows any of these folks. Or, if he is not an acquaintance, judge for yourself if the donor may still have the ability to influence the decision maker because of his position, reputation, or financial status.

Review the names and addresses of each of the people who make smaller donations to your effort. Donors with a widely recognized name or an address in a wealthy neighborhood may have the ability to influence decision makers. Place a call to each donor and hold a conversation similar to that described in the preceding paragraph.

You may wish to poll each of your supporters to determine if they may be influential. Design a questionnaire to cover all the possible factors that may allow a supporter to influence a decision maker. For example, you could list the decision makers you hope to influence and ask if the supporter is an acquaintance. Also, you could ask about place of employment and job title, as well as organizational affiliations and rank. The poll can be conducted either by mail, phone, or face-to-face.

Take a look at all your potential supporters, not just the folks who have contributed dollars or hours to your campaign. You may find someone who is sufficiently influential to justify a more concerted solicitation. Perhaps the person is not a supporter because she never responds to direct-mail or telemarketing solicitations, but may agree to lend her support after receiving a hand-written note or a call from one of your supporters with whom she is acquainted.

Once you have a compiled a list of your influential supporters, it will be easier to plan each of your tactics to win the support of decision makers. The initial correspondence in a letter-writing campaign could come from people who can influence the targeted decision maker. Or each of those attending an accountability session may be competent on the technical aspects of the issue as well as having the ability to influence the decision maker. And don't overlook influential supporters for fund-raising options. Perhaps one of these biggies sits on the board of a foundation or corporation you targeted for a grant request.

WHERE DO YOU GO FROM HERE?

In the next chapter, you will learn how to marshal the dollars, hours, and influence your supporters can provide, as well as everything else you have learned from other sections of this book, to formulate an overall strategy for your campaign.

9

Selecting the Best Strategy for Winning Your Campaign

Hopefully the question of strategy selection is rendered meaningless because: the owner has no intention of developing the property, the tract is unfit for development, or the real estate market is so poor that development is impractical. But if none of these enviable descriptions applies to your situation, you have three strategies to choose from:

1. Preserve the tract in a totally or partially undeveloped state.
2. Resolve specific issues.
3. Delay development.

Perhaps success lies not in a single strategy, but a combination of two or all three. The remainder of this chapter will help you to consider what you have learned and select the best strategy for winning your campaign.

SOME DEFINITIONS HELPFUL IN STRATEGY SELECTION

The following phrases embody a number of the concepts presented throughout this book. The phrases are intended to serve as a means of referring to these concepts in an abbreviated fashion to avoid the need of endlessly repeating the concepts in total.

A "crucial decision maker" is any individual whose support is essential to the implementation of a solution that will satisfy you.

An "effective legal option" is any form of litigation that has the potential to satisfy your concerns. The probability of success and the cost to pursue the option must be acceptable to you. Otherwise, the legal option is ineffective; it does not offer a reasonable likelihood of fulfilling your desires at a cost you can afford.

An "effective political option" will move a crucial decision maker to implement your preferred solution by demonstrating that his constituents support your cause. The effort involved in mobilizing support and the probability of success must be acceptable to you. If it is unlikely that you can mobilize a sufficient number of constituents to win the decision-maker's support, a political option is not effective.

"Mobilizing sufficient support" refers to your efforts to gain the money, volunteers, or influential allies needed to carry out an effective legal or political option. If you cannot raise sufficient funds to cover attorneys fees and other costs, legal action is not an effective option for satisfying your concerns. Or, if a decision-maker's constituents are opposed to your efforts, it is unlikely that you can use a political option to win his support.

LAND PRESERVATION

Will any of the following actions satisfy your concerns?
- Acquisition of the tract;
- Placing the tract under the protection of a conservation easement;
- Transferring either the density or development rights assigned to the tract to another site; or
- Developing only enough of the tract to generate the money needed to preserve a substantially greater area or those portions of the property of highest value.

Do you have the support of the crucial decision makers essential to the implementation of those actions that will satisfy your goals? Assuming that you responded to this question with a yes, then congratulations are in order. It appears that you have won a victory. But, if the answer is no, the next question is: Have you identified an effective legal or political option for gaining the support of each crucial decision maker? If the answer is yes, obviously you should begin carrying out the option as soon as you have mobilized sufficient support.

If you cannot identify an effective political or legal option for applying the four preservation approaches to the entirety of the tract, consider the benefits of using each approach to preserve a portion of the property. Would this approach meet your needs? If so, how would partial preservation alter the likelihood of gaining the support of crucial decision makers?

Should you find partial preservation to be a satisfactory solution, yet your chances of swaying crucial decision makers still seems remote, perhaps other actions may improve the probability of a successful outcome. For example, if decision makers refuse to acquire the tract due to the owner's high asking price, it may be possible to use delay to force the price down. Delay might also be used to forestall development until a decline in the real estate market lowers the value of the property. Or an effective legal option may be available for prompting government to condemn the property and reimburse the owner at a more equitable cost.

Finally, land preservation is most successful before an owner becomes committed to a development venture. Look around at other tracts of land where development may threaten your interests. Consider using all that you have learned to launch a preservation campaign now, before the owners of these tracts are no longer open to acquisition, an easement, or some other preservation option.

RESOLVING SPECIFIC ISSUES

Did your research reveal solutions that satisfy you and are compatible with the owner's plans for the development of his property? If the answer is yes, your campaign should be far easier to carry out when compared to the effort involved in land preservation or delaying development.

Do you need the support of decision makers, other than the property owner, to implement each solution? If so, has each crucial decision maker agreed to provide their support? If not, have you identified an effective legal or political option for gaining the support of each decision maker? If you answer yes to this question, begin carrying out the option as soon as you mobilize sufficient support.

What if you have a solution you like but the property owner refuses to implement? Read the next section on delaying development, and consider if you can use this strategy to gain the negotiating leverage needed to encourage the owner to implement the solution. Or look for decision makers who can force the owner to carry out the action you desire. It may then be necessary to identify an effective legal or political option to convince crucial decision makers to use their power to push the owner towards implementing your preferred solution.

DELAYING DEVELOPMENT

Development can be delayed by intervening in the owner's attempts to obtain the approvals and permits needed to begin developing his property. Delay may bring you:

- Greater negotiating leverage with the owner;
- The time needed to implement more permanent solutions, such as lowering the development potential of the tract through a change in zoning; or
- Driving up costs to the point where the owner is forced to abandon the development proposal.

Before launching a delaying action, there are a few questions to consider. Does delay offer a viable strategy for satisfying your concerns on both a short- and long-term basis? Delay may succeed in thwarting the issuance of an essential permit today, but what about a year from now? Are you prepared to launch a campaign to defeat a new development proposal every few years or so?

Generally, the more outrageous the development proposal, the easier it is to kill the venture. As the impact upon the community increases and the benefits dwindle in comparison, your chances for defeating a development project improve. But the reverse may also be true. The more a proposal matches projects routinely approved in your area, the less the likelihood of killing the project. Usually, delay is most effective when used to bring about either solutions to specific development issues or a land preservation option.

If delaying development will allow you to satisfy your concerns, the next question is: Have you identified an effective legal or political option that will result in sufficient delay? Generally, it is best to launch a delaying action on a number of fronts. In other words, use legal and/or political action to delay the issuance of as many approvals and permits as possible. This multifaceted attack will increase your potential for achieving your goals through delay.

If you cannot find an effective option for delaying development and neither preservation nor solutions to specific issues will meet your needs, perhaps you should re-examine your goals. Given all that you have learned, are your goals realistic? If none of the three strategies will be satisfactory, it may be that your goals are unattainable. Or, consider other strategies, such as changing the law, working through those who are providing the property owner's financial backing, or attempting to scare off potential buyers.

THE SCENIC WOODLAND:
AN EXAMPLE OF STRATEGY SELECTION

The following example will illustrate how a group might go about researching options and selecting the most effective strategy for winning their campaign. This example also demonstrates how to develop a plan of action, which should describe all the steps you intend to take to reach your goals. The plan of action shows what must be done and by when, who will do it, what resources they will need, and how, when, and where these resources will be found. Developing this plan will help you to identify all the specific actions that must be taken to successfully carry out your strategy. The plan of action forces one to think through an entire campaign. This exercise can help you to distinguish a realistic strategy from what may be little more than wishful thinking.

The Scenic Woodland

The scenic woodland is a 100-acre parcel located next to Forest Hills—a bedroom community of several hundred homes situated on quarter-acre lots. The woodland is one of the last undeveloped tracts in the area. It serves as sort of an unofficial park for children and adult nature enthusiasts.

The Forest Hills Association is concerned about the woodland. Development has steadily encroached up to the borders of the property. Four members of the association have decided that they had better act now, before the bulldozers start turning the tract into a non-woodland. The four members are: Judy, who is the president of the association and an accountant; Jim, a computer programmer, who lives next to the woodland; Ted, who also lives next to the woodland and owns a sporting goods store; and Mary, the association's zoning committee chairperson and a school teacher.

Judy invited the other three association members to join her for coffee one evening to discuss the woodland. As the group sits down to Judy's kitchen table, Mary tells the group that she has learned that the woodland is zoned for quarter-acre homesites. She also knows that the owner, Mrs. Gerald, is quite elderly and still lives on the property. Mary has also heard that, while Mrs. Gerald would like to keep the woodland rural, her two children may have other plans once the property is theirs.

After discussing the issue, the four association members list the following damages that might result from development of the woodland and one benefit derived from retaining the site in its current condition.

1. Judy fears that part of the traffic generated by the development will travel along the rather narrow road she lives on.

2. Mary says that the local high school is presently at capacity, but the county projects a drop in enrollment in five years.

3. Ted is concerned that pollution from the site will damage the trout stream flowing through the woodland.

4. Jim pointed out that the meadow along the trout stream is frequented by Forest Hill residents who like to fish, wade, and picnic.

When stated as goals, the four items listed above appear as:

1. To ensure that traffic from the development can be accommodated on adjacent roads in a safe, efficient manner.

2. To ensure that schools are adequate for both the children who live in the area already and those who will come from the development.

3. To ensure that those who will live in the development will be able to enjoy a high-quality trout stream.

4. To ensure that the meadow continues to be a pleasant setting for wading, picnicking, and similar pursuits.

Judy and the other association members have decided that the ideal solution would be to turn the woodland into a park. This solution would satisfy all four goals. They have elected to write a letter to Mrs. Gerald, thanking her for allowing Forest Hill residents to use her property, and to ask for an opportunity to talk to her about the future of the tract. In the letter, which will be found on page 13, they described the goals they hoped to achieve.

The wording of the goals clearly showed that the association had not assumed that development of the tract would inevitably be harmful. In fact, the goal statements implied that development and the association's welfare were compatible. This positive approach will increase the likelihood of a cooperative response from Mrs. Gerald. After all, the association does not know if Mrs. Gerald intends to develop her property. If she is committed to development, her willingness to cooperate will be greater if the association is open to development as well. On the other hand, a "development is bad" attitude on the association's part would probably offend the property owner and result in either a refusal to meet or, at best, a lukewarm reception.

Mary agreed to follow up on the letter by placing a phone call to

Mrs. Gerald. After chatting briefly, the owner said she would be delighted to meet. Mrs. Gerald also mentioned her own uncertainty about the woodland. She says its really up to her children, both of whom live out of state.

All four association representatives attended the meeting, which was held at Mrs. Gerald's home. The aging widow said that she had always hoped to retain the 100-acre woodland in a natural state. Both she and her deceased husband had been avid bird watchers. She fondly recalled long summer afternoons spent walking along the trout stream and the moments of great delight when she and her husband encountered an unusual bird.

Mrs. Gerald also spoke of some very practical considerations. As the surrounding area has developed, the assessed value of her property has skyrocketed, along with the taxes she pays on the land. Her husband had left her just enough money to keep up with the taxes and other living expenses, but not much more. Although a number of people have approached her about selling the land for development, Mrs. Gerald has declined their offers, some of which were quite sizeable. One developer had even offered her $20,000 an acre or $2 million for the entire woodland!

Neither of Mrs. Gerald's children wished to live on the property. Both had careers and families in other parts of the country. She doubted that they could afford the taxes and upkeep once the land became theirs. Frankly, she did not really know what her children would do with the property. There had been some talk about selling the land to cover college tuition for her grandchildren and the many other expenses associated with raising a family. But her children disliked the idea of destroying the woodland as much as she did.

After thanking Mrs. Gerald for her time, the party of four adjourned the meeting to a nearby restaurant. Over coffee, they exchanged small talk while searching for a way of dealing with the rather morbid question: "What happens when Mrs. Gerald is no longer around?"

It seemed fairly certain that development would not occur until the children became the owners. Mrs. Gerald's future heirs would have few options other then selling the woodland, and a development company would surely offer the best price.

Fortunately, since development was at least a few years off, the overcrowded conditions at the high school would probably subside before space was needed for additional students. That still left the other three concerns: traffic, the trout stream, and the meadow.

A park still seemed the best solution for everyone concerned. The questions were:

1. Would anyone be interested in buying the property for use as a park?

2. If so, would Mrs. Gerald and her children agree to sell the property for this purpose?

The second question was easy to answer. From what they learned during the meeting with the elderly widow, the answer was probably yes as far as Mrs. Gerald was concerned. The answer from her children would probably depend on the amount offered. Although it surely would not be as much as a developer might offer, the children did share their mother's desire to preserve the woodland. The children might accept an amount closer to what the parks department or some other preservation group might offer.

To answer the first question, the four association members decided to talk to the county parks department and to try to find a foundation or land trust that might be interested in the woodland. Their first plan of action consisted of the following steps.

1. Mary and Jim will meet with the director of the county parks department.

2. Ted will research foundations by going to the "foundation center" located in the county's main library. He will talk to the executive director or president of each foundation that has made grants for the acquisition of parkland in the state.

3. Judy will call The Land Trust Exchange to get a list of land trusts that have acquired land in the state. She will talk to the principal staff person with each land trust to learn if they might have any interest in acquiring the woodland.

4. The four will meet in three weeks to share their findings.

After completing their research, the association members again gathered around the table in Judy's kitchen. Ted identified three foundations that have purchased land within the state. Two said their land acquisition funds were committed for the foreseeable future, and the third said that they only purchased historically significant land. Ted said he made a call to the local historical society, but did not come up with anything useful. Society officials said that Mrs. Gerald's home and the immediate lot might qualify for the national historic register, but not the surrounding hundred acres. After speaking with the foundation again, Ted learned that they might consider a joint preservation effort if some other agency purchased the adjoining land.

Judy learned of one land trust active in their area. That trust only purchases land that supports a "unique ecological habitat." When she asked a trust staff person what that meant, none of the examples offered seemed to match the woodland. But the official said they would be interested if the association found an endangered plant or animal on the property. Ted said he had an uncle who was a pretty rare bird, what if they planted him on the site? Judy brought the conversation back to a serious note by saying that she spoke to a biologist who offered to comb the woodland for endangered critters for $500. No one laughed.

Mary and Jim, who had been strangely quiet, broke into grins and said they had good news and bad news to announce. Ted and Judy requested the former. Looking at Ted and Judy, Mary said "The parks director was quite helpful. He predicted that the foundations and the land trust would say pretty much what you two just reported. The director also said that the county has plans to buy the woodland, or rather a piece of it." The expressions on both Ted and Judy's face went quickly from ecstasy to puzzlement.

Jim chimed in, "The director said that the land along the trout stream is shown as a future stream valley park on the county's master plan. In fact, the director has put the money in the county's budget several times to buy the valley. But the county council has never approved the funding. He said that invariably some council member bumped the valley so another piece of land could be bought. The director thought that the council could be persuaded to approve the purchase of the valley if the councilman representing our area supported the move and a lot of people called for the acquisition."

"So that's the good news," Jim said, as he gave Mary a look that urged her to continue with the not-so-good news.

"The director," Mary began with a somber expression, "told us that the county is prohibited by law from paying more than the appraised value for property. The land in the valley is appraised at $5,000 an acre. That's one-fourth of the highest offer a developer made Mrs. Gerald for her land!" Nodding at Jim, Mary continued, "we told the director of the offer Mrs. Gerald had received. We said we were uncertain if Mrs. Gerald and her children would accept a figure so far below the offer made by development interests. The director said the county might have another appraisal made. If the developer's offer is real, the appraisal should reflect the greater value. Otherwise the county might go a bit higher, but not by much." "Finally," Mary said with a note of hesitation, "the director sort of hinted that the county could force Mrs. Gerald to sell at a lower price through a condemnation proceeding."

Everyone winced at this last statement. The thought of dragging that nice lady into court was most distasteful.

"There's one more piece of bad news," Mary said. "The director showed us a map of the proposed stream valley park. The county intends to acquire only the land in the valley, which is about one-third of the total woodland."

After discussing the results of their research for half an hour more, the four association members reached the following conclusions concerning their strategy.

1. If the stream valley became a park, that would protect the meadow for the community's use.

2. If one-third of the woodland became a park, this would reduce the number of homes that could be built on the remainder of the tract. The reduction in homes would also reduce the amount of traffic and water pollution resulting from the development of Mrs. Gerald's property. But the reduction may not be enough to protect the quality of the trout stream and to maintain safe conditions along Judy's narrow street.

3. The association should look into other options for dealing with traffic and pollution.

Following is the association's second plan of action.

1. Jim will talk to Mrs. Gerald to find out if she would sell the 33 acres in the stream valley for $5,000 per acre instead of the $20,000 offered by development interests.

2. If Mrs. Gerald expresses a willingness to sell at that price, or something "slightly" higher, Jim will meet with the parks director to see if he would put the money in the department's budget proposal.

3. If Jim is successful, Mary will meet with their County Councilman, Dan Taylor, to see if he will support the effort to acquire the valley.

4. Ted will talk to the state trout biologist and other experts to learn if the reduction in pollution, which would occur if one-third of the land were not developed, would be sufficient to preserve the quality of the creek.

5. Judy will talk to the director of the county highway department to find out what options might be available for dealing with the traffic question.

Again, since all five steps of the plan of action involve research, there will not be any significant costs in terms of volunteers or dollars. The four association members automatically assume the burden for the minuscule expense.

Ten days later Jim announced that Mrs. Gerald and her children would accept the offer for the valley land. Initially, Mrs. Gerald's son thought the family should receive at least half of what the developer had offered; $10,000 an acre. But Mrs. Gerald and her daughter figured they would make more than enough off the other 67 acres and preserving the valley was worth the loss. The son relented.

Jim's talk with the parks director also went quite well. The director agreed to place the necessary funds in a special budget request to be submitted to the county council next month. The council would probably vote on the budget request in six to eight weeks.

Mary had a long talk with Councilman Taylor who agreed to support the effort when the department's special budget request came before the council. He conducted an informal poll of other members of the council to see if a majority of the seven legislators would approve the measure. He learned that Councilman Scott would vote against the request. Some time back, Councilman Taylor had encouraged three other members of the council to kill a pork-barrel project that would have benefited a large contributor to Councilman Scott's last election campaign. Two other councilmen, who frequently vote the same as Scott, were "skeptical" about the measure. But another two councilmen thought they would vote for the budget request, and the seventh member is undecided. So, at this point, there are probably three votes against, three votes for, and one undecided. Four votes are needed to win.

The state trout biologist told Ted that the reduction in the number of homes, street area, and land disturbance would certainly help but would not guarantee continuance of the high quality of the stream. The biologist said that a recent study showed that stormwater runoff from developed lands was particularly harmful to trout. The study recommended that land draining to trout streams remain undeveloped or, if that is not possible, then all stormwater runoff from developed lands should flow to something called an "infiltration" device. An infiltration device is a stone-filled pit that holds runoff until it can soak into adjacent soils. Most of the pollution is removed as the runoff travels through the soil. Finally, the biologist said that county development review officials were reluctant to require infiltration devices; they feel the devices are too difficult and expensive to maintain.

Judy discovered that the county highway officials were also concerned that additional traffic on her street might cause a safety problem. But the officials felt the street might safely handle some increase in traffic, therefore, they refused to prohibit the extension of Mary's street and the increase in auto traffic that would follow. The officials also resisted Mary's efforts to get them to say how much of a traffic increase they might allow. Instead, they preferred to wait for the results of a traffic study a developer would be required to submit in order to receive approval to extend the street.

After sharing their findings, Ted made an impassioned plea to expand the park effort to the entire woodland. He presented a convincing case that complete acquisition was the only way to guarantee the survival of the trout stream. While the other three agreed with Ted's argument, they also reminded him of what Mrs. Gerald and Councilman Taylor had said. It will probably be a struggle to get the Council to approve $5,000 for 33 acres. Mrs. Gerald and her family will demand a larger sum, perhaps $20,000 an acre, for the land outside the valley. It just doesn't seem likely that they could convince Taylor, much less the entire council, to go for the whole woodland. In the end, Ted agreed to go along with the stream valley park approach, provided the association would insist upon the use of infiltration devices to control stormwater runoff.

For obvious reasons, Judy was not satisfied with the unresolved question of additional traffic on her street. Yet, until a developer conducted the traffic study, there did not seem to be a great deal she could do about it. The association members considered the possibility of doing their own traffic study. But why go to the expense of hiring a traffic expert when some future developer would likely do his own study anyway? Would it not be better to wait for the developer's study to be completed, then hire an expert, at a far lower cost, to review the results?

Based upon the strategy outlined above, the association's third plan of action consisted of the following steps.

1. Judy attended a countywide gathering of community organization leaders a few months ago. She recalled meeting the presidents of several groups with a large membership in the district of the undecided councilman. She will ask each of the presidents of these groups to participate in an accountability session with the councilman. Judy will also invite the following people to attend the session; the parks director, Councilman Taylor, and her attorney, who happens to support the stream valley park and is a golfing buddy of the undecided councilman.

2. Jim has accepted responsibility for coordinating a mass turnout at the hearing the council will hold on the special budget request for the acquisition of the stream valley park. The association would like to get at least 200 people at the hearing. His objective will be to get a good showing from all councilmanic districts, except that of Scott. Jim will focus his efforts, in order of priority, on the districts of the following council members: the undecided member, the two probable "yes-voting" members, and the two members who will likely vote no. Jim will execute the following actions to pack the hearing.

a. Request help from all the citizen groups supporting the issue who have membership in the six council districts (Ted knew several fishing clubs with members countywide, Judy said she would call selected community groups to ask for their support, and Mary belongs to the Sierra Club, which has a large membership throughout the county);

b. Each supporting group will be asked to allow the association to make a mailing to their members about the issue;

c. Supporting groups would also be asked to provide a list containing the name, address, and phone number of each member receiving a mailing;

d. Ted will handle the recruitment of volunteers to participate in a telemarketing effort to encourage recipients of the mailing to either attend the hearing or write a letter to their councilman (the mailing described in "b.", above, gave specifics on the hearing and enough detail to allow the supporter to write a good letter; letters were to be sent to Jim so he could track the response rate and pass the letters on to the appropriate council member), and

e. Judy would ask Councilman Taylor to periodically poll the other members of the council to assess the effect of the letter campaign.

3. Judy agreed to develop a budget for the effort if Mary will coordinate a fund raiser to generate the money needed to cover the cost of the mailings and telemarketing. After seeing the budget, Mary decided that she can probably meet expenses by doing telemarketing within Forest Hills.

4. Judy and Ted will do a joint accountability session with the County Executive if the association wins the battle for park funding. The added political clout resulting from a victory in the park battle would give Ted and Judy, as representatives of the association, a better chance of winning the Executive's commitment to seriously consider infiltration devices and strict limits on additional traffic along Judy's street.

The budget produced by Judy described the following expenses and income.

EXPENSES

Mailing to 1,600 to get 200 at hearing:	
Printing (two-page letter)	$ 96
Envelopes	50
Postage (bulk rate)	160
Telemarketing to 1,600:	
Telephone Costs ($0.10/call)	160
Pledge Packets (200)	90
TOTAL	$556

INCOME

Telemarketing to 400 residents of Forest Hills	
50% response rate × 70% pledge fulfillment	
rate × $20/pledge =	$2,800

On the next page, you will find the association's time line for the steps described above. The time line covers the eight-week period from the moment the association agreed to execute the third plan of action to the date of the council hearing.

Once the third plan of action is successfully completed, there will probably be at least one more round of steps. The fourth plan of action will focus on two concerns: 1) making certain the council and the parks department make good on the acquisition of the stream valley, and 2) making certain the Executive follows through with his probable commitment to resolve the traffic and the stormwater/trout stream issues.

The example of the Scenic Woodland is little more than a rough sketch—an abbreviated illustration—of how a real campaign might

Save the Scenic Woodland Campaign Time Line

	Week							
	1	2	3	4	5	6	7	8
Step 1: Accountability session								
Request participation of other community group presidents, the parks director, Councilman Taylor, and golfing buddy	x							
Request opportunity to meet with undecided councilman; say who's coming		x						
Confirm meeting with participants			x					
Hold meeting				x				
Assess impact and modify strategy					x			
Step 2: Mass turnout for hearing								
Request support of groups	x							
Groups make decision on request	x	x						
Once number of supporters is known, have mailing contents printed		x	x	x				
Make mailing to supporters					x			
Mailing received						x		
Recruit volunteers for telemarketing to generate letters/hearing, turnout/fund-raising	x	x						
Secure telemarketing facility and other items essential for calling	x	x	x	x	x			
Receive calling lists		x						
Make calls for turnout, letters, and funds						x	x	
Check status with Councilman Taylor				x		x	x	x
Step 3: Fund-raising								
Send letter to Forest Hills residents explaining issue	x	x	x	x				
Make calls requesting funds			x	x				
Most of funds received					x	x	x	x
Step 4: County executive								
Assess logic of going forward with accountability session								x

evolve and play out. But, the example does indicate how research provides the basis for identifying the best ways of attaining one's goals and how specific steps are taken in a steady progression towards the completion of a strategy.

So, once you reach this point, there's nothing more to learn. Well, that's not quite true. Once you win a commitment that will lead to victory, the next step is to make certain that somebody makes good on the commitment. The next chapter will explain "How to Make Victory Last."

10

How to Make
Victory Last!

So what happens after you've won iron-clad commitments from all the right folks to carry out actions that will satisfy your goals? Do you go fishing, take a vacation, get to know your family again? Well, maybe, but don't take too much time off. Now you must make certain that all those folks deliver on their promises!

Once you have won a commitment, you should find out what steps will be taken to make good on the commitment. Monitor those responsible for taking each step to ensure that steady progress is made towards the attainment of your goals.

Once the goal is finally achieved, develop a strategy for ensuring that a lack of maintenance or the simple effects of time do not erode your success.

Perhaps an example would help to demonstrate how a victory can dwindle with time.

Most construction activities are regulated through a permitting and inspection process. The purpose of permitting and inspections is to protect public health, safety, and welfare. When the permitting/ inspection process fails to work, the public is jeopardized.

To obtain the necessary permits, the developer must submit a plan showing how he intends to complete tasks such as plumbing, wiring, insulation, and environmental protection. If the plan complies with local standards and specifications, the developer receives a permit to proceed with each task. A government inspector will visit the building site periodically to ensure that the developer completes each task in accordance with the plan he submitted. If the builder is not in compliance, the inspector can take several actions designed to achieve compliance. These actions may lead to a fine, imprisonment, or closing the job down.

Erosion and sediment control is one of those aspects of construction that is frequently regulated through a permit and inspection process. The intent of erosion and sediment control is to reduce the volume of mud washed into nearby waterways from barren construction site soils. Without effective control, the mud pollution from a typical construction site can damage three miles of downstream waters, and a century may be required for the damaged waterway to fully recover. Generally, for each dollar the developer spends keeping mud on the construction site, at least $100 in damages are prevented.

Normally, a developer will be required to prepare an erosion and sediment control plan. The plan details all the steps the developer will take to keep mud on the site. The plan usually calls for a system of ditches placed along the downslope perimeter of the site to capture all rainwater runoff from exposed soils. The ditches carry mud-laden runoff waters to a pond or some other device where eroded soil, suspended in runoff, will settle. If the developer's plan complies with local standards and specifications for erosion and sediment control, a permit is issued and site clearance may begin.

Government inspection of the site begins shortly after trees and other vegetation are cleared and soils are exposed to erosive forces. The inspector walks the entire site to determine if the developer has installed all the erosion and sediment control measures shown on his approved plan. Should the inspector find that a measure is missing or failing due to a lack of maintenance, an order may be issued to the developer requiring immediate corrective action.

At first glance, it would appear that the permit and inspection process would be an effective way to ensure that measures intended to protect the public are fully implemented throughout the development process. But appearances can be deceiving.

In Maryland, the "birthplace" of erosion and sediment control, only 15 to 50 percent of all construction sites comply with the plan approved for the site. And the situation is made worse by the ineffectiveness of the control devices that are installed. Many control measures, such as ponds and straw bales, only keep a third to half the mud on the site. The other half to two-thirds flows off site to pollute nearby waters!

In Chapter 9, Ted was concerned about the effects of development of the scenic woodland upon the trout stream. He talked to the state trout biologist who told Ted about stormwater runoff from the site after construction is completed and all the exposed soils are covered with lawns, homes, and asphalt. Ted had not considered erosion and sediment control during the construction phase. Perhaps he and the biologist assumed that mud would be adequately controlled. If Ted's stream happened to be in Maryland, chances are quite good that the trout would not survive the construction phase. Ted might have won the battle for infiltration devices, but mud would have caused the loss of his favorite trout-fishing waters!

The moral of this tale of woe is: "You get what you inspect, not what you expect." Once you have won a commitment to preserve a tract of land or to resolve a specific development issue, begin monitoring progress. Find out what steps must be taken to:

- Make preservation a reality; or
- Fully implement your preferred solution for each issue.

Then, follow-up on each step to make certain it is carried through to fruition.

Let's continue a bit further with the example of Ted's trout stream and mud pollution. The author has just magically transformed the situation described in the previous chapter. If you were to read about the scenic woodland again, you would learn that the state biologist clued Ted into stormwater and mud. When Ted and Judy met with the County Executive, they won commitments for infiltration of stormwater, traffic safeguards, and mud pollution control laws. In fact, Ted called for the use of straw mulch and grass seedings to improve upon the effectiveness of the sediment ponds. If straw and grass seed is spread over exposed soils, the amount of mud leaving the site is reduced by 90 percent or more! Ted convinced the Executive to require the use of straw mulch and grass seed on the scenic woodland construction site. Way to go, Ted!

And this gets even better yet. It just so happens that there is a citizen group in Maryland called Save Our Streams (SOS). This group shows citizens how to evaluate the quality of mud pollution control measures on construction sites. They also show people how to organize and lobby for better control of mud pollution. Campaigns mounted by SOS volunteers have produced a fivefold improvement in the quality of mud pollution control!

After going through an SOS mud pollution control training program, Ted begins monitoring the scenic woodland development site. He catches several violations of the erosion and sediment control plan. These are reported to the county inspector. The inspector visits the site, confirms Ted's findings, and issues an order calling for corrective action. The corrections are made just before a thunderstorm rolls across the site. But the straw mulch and the ponds keep the mud on the site and out of the trout stream. That Ted, what a guy!

Enough levity for the moment. Save Our Streams has not only trained hundreds of volunteers in mud pollution control, they have also shown people how to monitor all the other aspects of development that may harm aquatic resources. Typically, sites monitored by SOS volunteers have a far milder impact upon nearby waterways when compared to other sites.

What Save Our Streams does to minimize the environmental impacts of development can also be done for the other damages associated with building activity. Again, follow up is the only way to be certain that your goals become reality, and stay that way. So postpone the fishing trip and the vacation, ask the wife and kids for a bit more time, and develop a strategy for ensuring that your goals are fully achieved.

Develop a strategy for monitoring the progress of each action that will lead to the attainment of your goals. Find out how effective the action has been in attaining goals similar to yours in the past. If the action has been effective, then great, you can relax a bit. But, if the action works only part of the time, you have a problem. If you cannot find a way to guarantee that the action will be effective, perhaps another mechanism should be pursued.

Consider what options will be open to you if government, the property owner, or the developer fails to implement an action. What steps must you take to correct the situation? Can you realistically take these steps? For example, covenants are a popular method of imposing special restrictions upon a proposed development venture. A covenant is placed in the deed and requires the property owner to take specific actions during site development. Perhaps the covenant requires that a certain number of trees remain undisturbed or that a buffer be placed along a property line or waterway. On the surface, a covenant may seem like a great way for a community group to ensure that a project is compatible with their interests, but is the covenant enforceable? And who has the power to enforce the covenant? And will the community group have difficulty in getting the enforcement entity to act? And if the community has the enforcement responsibility, how much will it cost? In Maryland, it may cost $5,000 to take legal action when a covenant is violated!

So, before you resume a normal life, make certain that your wins will become a reality and will continue to protect your interests once you've left for the mountains.

CHAPTER

11

Dealing With Development on a Community Level

In this chapter, an approach will be presented for resolving development issues on more than one site, perhaps tackling issues that affect a township, a river basin, a county, or a state.

Like the process illustrated for a single tract, the approach begins by identifying damages resulting from development. Next, the benefits are listed that may result from preserving land in an undeveloped state or by reducing the intensity of development. Finally, damages and benefits are formed into goal statements.

Once goals have been identified, the search begins for options to achieve those goals. But the search takes on a somewhat different character from that employed when you considered only one tract. The options must have the ability to solve development issues on a grander scale.

For example, if you completed the research outlined in Chapter 4—How to Preserve Land—you probably learned that preservation funds are rather limited. While you might succeed in preserving one tract through acquisition, the funds simply are not there to purchase more than a few potential development sites. In this event, you may wish to investigate the possibility of:

- Expanding the amount of acquisition funds;
- Enhancing the benefits property owners receive through easements;
- Expanding the authority of local government to use a transfer of density/development rights to preserve important tracts of land;

- Encouraging local foundations to allocate more of their budget to land preservation projects;
- Forming a land trust to focus on land protection issues of concern to you; or
- Encouraging the local government to foster market conditions favoring limited development ventures.

Perhaps the problem is not so much a lack of funding, or a paucity of other preservation options, but more one of exposure. Maybe the existing easement programs are good and more property owners would preserve their land, if only they knew of the program and the benefits of entering into an easement agreement. You might find that several of those who own property in your area would agree to an easement once you explained the benefits and lent a hand with the leg-work involved in securing the easement.

A similar broad approach should be taken with specific development issues. If you feel that current development regulations allow practices that adversely affect public health, safety, or welfare, perhaps the regulations should be changed. Or maybe the problem is one of inspection and enforcement. In Chapter 10—How to Make Victory Last—you learned that one citizen group, Maryland Save Our Streams, won sweeping improvements in the enforcement of erosion and sediment control regulations. The same may be done with other inspection and enforcement programs affecting your interests.

Once you have identified options for solving a broad development issue, proceed with the process for identifying those who have the power to carry out each option. This process was described in Chapter 7—Encouraging Decision Makers to Support Your Cause. Once you have identified decision makers who have the power to carry out each option, determine which you can influence. Then use the tactics described in Chapter 7 to encourage decision makers to act on your behalf. The suggestions offered in Chapter 8—Mobilizing Public Support for Your Cause—and Chapter 9—Bringing It All Together Into a Winning Strategy—will help you to gain the resources you need and to plan out a strategy for a successful campaign.

What if no one has the power to implement options that will solve a problem? This may occur when attempting to expand land preservation efforts or to tighten development regulations. Current law may prohibit the option you have proposed. Or a more ambitious acquisition program may require an unpopular tax increase.

Further research should indicate if the law can be changed. Even after you have researched the issue extensively, you may learn that no one is certain if a stronger law will stand up if challenged through court action.

You may find decision makers agreeing that a more ambitious acquisition effort is warranted, yet no government official is willing to take the risk of angering the voters by proposing a tax increase. Neither will an official wish to cut some other government program to free tax dollars for the purchase of land. It may take a referendum (described in Chapter 7) and a massive organizing campaign to drag politicians kicking and screaming to an agreement on a tax increase.

Before you propose such an ambitious campaign, take a look around at past efforts of a similar scale. Try to find efforts that resemble the one you are contemplating. Talk to the people who organized those efforts. Find out what the campaign cost in terms of money, volunteers, and the organizer's time. What mistakes did they make? What worked well for them? If they won, what produced the victory? A defeat is an equally valuable learning opportunity; what caused the loss? Is it conceivable that you can generate an equivalent amount of dollars and volunteers? How much of your life must you sacrifice in order to free the time it will take to lead the campaign? Are the benefits really worth the effort? These and many other questions should be answered before embarking on a large-scale campaign.

Although thorough research, good planning, and a well thought-out strategy is always important, these three items become even more crucial as the scale of a campaign increases. So think big, but proceed carefully.

References and Sources of Information

CHAPTER 3. TRY THE EASY SOLUTIONS FIRST

Negotiations: The Art of Getting What You Want, Michael Schatzki, 230 pp., Signet Books, 1633 Broadway, New York, NY 10019.

Power Play: How to Deal Like a Lawyer in Person-to-Person Confrontations, John M. Striker and Andrew O. Shapiro, 351 pp., Dell Publishing Co., 1 Dag Hammarskjold Plaza, New York, NY 10017.

CHAPTER 4. HOW TO PRESERVE LAND

For information on land trusts, conservation easements, and other voluntary land protection measures contact: The Land Trust Exchange, 1017 Duke St., Alexandria, VA 22314, 703-683-7778.

For information on foundations: The Foundation Center, 79 Fifth Ave., New York, NY 10003, 1-800-424-9836.

CHAPTER 5. RESOLVING SPECIFIC DEVELOPMENT ISSUES

Experts: A User's Guide, Will Collette, 29 pp., $4.75, Citizens Clearinghouse for Hazardous Waste, Inc., P.O. Box 926, Arlington, VA 22216, 703-276-7070.

Research Guide for Leaders, Will Collette, 19 pp., $3.50, Citizens Clearinghouse for Hazardous Waste, Inc., P.O. Box 926, Arlington, VA 22216, 703-276-7070.

Endangered Species

Endangered and Threatened Wildlife and Plants, 32 pp., U.S. Fish and Wildlife Service, Publications Unit, Washington, DC 20240.

Endangered Means There's Still Time, 33 pgs., U.S. Fish and Wildlife Service, Publications Unit, Washington, DC 20240.

Noise

Information on levels of environmental noise requisite to protect public health and welfare with an adequate margin of safety, 1974, U.S. Environmental Protection Agency, Washington, DC 20460.

Septic Systems

Design Manual: Onsite Wastewater Treatment and Disposal Systems, 391 pp., U.S. Environmental Protection Agency, Water Programs Operations, EPA 625/1-80-012, Washington, DC 20460.

Sewerlines

Handbook for Sewer System Evaluation and Rehabilitation, 150 pp., U.S. Environmental Protection Agency, Water Programs Operations, 430/9-75-21, Washington, DC 20460.

Soil Erosion

The Mud Pollution Action Guide: In Search of Private Eyes, 14 pp., Save Our Streams, 258 Scotts Manor Drive, Glen Burnie, MD 21061, 301-969-0084.

Stormwater and Flooding

Effects of Urbanization Upon Aquatic Resources, Richard Klein, 71 pp., Save Our Streams, 258 Scotts Manor Drive, Glen Burnie, MD 21061, 301-969-0084.

Controlling Urban Runoff: A Practical Manual for Planning and Designing Urban Best Management Practices, Thomas R. Schueler, 275 pgs., $40, Metropolitan Washington Council of Governments, 1875 Eye St., NW, Suite 200, Washington, DC 20006, 202-223-6800.

Urban Hydrology for Small Watersheds, USDA Soil Conservation Service, available from National Technical Information Service, Springfield, VA 22161, use order number PB87-101580.

Traffic

AASHTO Guide Specifications for Highway Construction, $20, American Association of State Highway and Transportation Officials, 444 N. Capital St., NW, Washington, DC 20001, 202-624-5800.

Wells

Groundwater Hydrology, Herman Bouwer, 480 pp., McGraw-Hill Book Co., New York, NY 10020.

Wetlands

Our National Wetland Heritage: A Protection Guidebook, Jon A. Kusler, 167 pp., Environmental Law Institute, 1616 P St., NW, Washington, DC 20036, 202-328-5150.

Wetlands, William A. Niering, 638 pp., The Audubon Society Nature Guides, National Audubon Socie-

ty, 950 Third Ave., New York, NY 10022.

CHAPTER 6. DO YOU NEED A LAWYER?

User's Guide to Lawyers, Will Collette, 31 pp., $5.75, Citizens Clearinghouse for Hazardous Waste, Inc., P.O. Box 926, Arlington, VA 22216, 703-276-7070.

CHAPTER 7. ENCOURAGING DECISION MAKERS TO SUPPORT YOUR CAUSE

Community Power Structure: A Study of Decision Makers, Floyd Hunter, 297 pp., Anchor Books, Doubleday & Co., N.Y., NY 10103.

Practical Politics, Maryann Mahaffey and John W. Hanks, 260 pp., National Association of Social Workers, 301-565-0333 Silver Spring, MD 20910.

Rules for Radicals, Saul Alinsky, Vintage Books, Random House New York, NY 10022.

Leadership Handbook on Hazardous Waste, Lois Marie Gibbs and Will Collette, 59 pgs., Citizens Clearinghouse for Hazardous Waste, Inc., P.O. Box 926, Arlington, VA 22216, 703-276-7070.

Midwest Academy Organizing Manual, 270 pp., $40, Midwest Academy, 225 W. Ohio St., Suite 250, Chicago, IL 60610, 312-645-6010.

Motivating Volunteers, Larry F. Moore, 261 pp., Vancouver Volunteer Centre, 1625 W. 8th Ave., Vancouver, BC V6J 1T9, Canada.

Volunteers Today: Finding, Training, and Working With Them, Harriet H. Naylor, 198 pp., Dryden Association, Box 363, Dryden, NY 13053.

How People Get Power, Si Kahn, 128 pp., McGraw-Hill, Inc., New York, NY 10020.

The Effective Management of Volunteer Programs, Marlene Wilson, 197 pp., Volunteer Management Association, 279 S. Cedar Brook Rd., Boulder, CO 80302.

CHAPTER 8. MOBILIZING PUBLIC SUPPORT FOR YOUR CAUSE

Fund Raising

Fund Raising for Social Change, Kim Klein, 1985, 208 pp., CRG Press, P.O. Box 42120, Washington, DC 20015, 202-223-2400.

The Grass Roots Fund-Raising Book, Joan Flanagan, 1982, 344 pp., $11.95, Beaverbooks, Ltd., 150 Lesmill Road, Don Mills, Ontario M3B 2T5, Canada.

How to Raise and Manage Money, Will Collette, 55 pp., $6.50, Citizens Clearinghouse for Hazardous Waste, Inc., P.O. Box 926, Arlington, VA 22216, 703-276-7070.

Grassroots Fund-Raising Journal, a bimonthly publication, $20/year, Grassroots Fund-Raising Journal, 517 Union Ave., Knoxville, TN 37902, 615-637-6624.

Major Gifts Campaign, 20 pp., $7,

Grassroots Fund-Raising Journal, 517 Union Ave., Knoxville, TN 37902, 615-637-6624.

Telepledge: The Complete Guide to Mail-Phone Fund Raising, Louis A. Schultz, 201 pp., $68, The Taft Group, 301-816-0210 Rockville, MD 20852.

Foundations

The Foundation Center, 79 Fifth Ave., New York, NY 10003, 1-800-424-9836.

Other Topics

The Successful Volunteer Organization, Joan Flanagan, 376 pp., Contemporary Books, Inc., 180 N. Michigan Ave., Chicago, IL 60601.

How to Make Meetings Work, Michael Doyle and David Straus, 298 pp., The Berkley Publishing Group, 200 Madison Ave., New York, NY 10016.

Practical Publicity: How to Boost Any Cause, David Tedone, 1985, 179 pp., $8.95, The Harvard Common Press, Boston, MA 02118.

CHAPTER 10. HOW TO MAKE VICTORY LAST

For further information on Save Our Streams, write to 258 Scotts Manor Dr., Glen Burnie, MD 21061, or call 301-969-0084.

How to Fund Your Campaign Through Telemarketing

Of all the fund-raising techniques the author has used since 1970, none has performed so consistently well as telemarketing. And this statement is particularly true for campaigns to preserve land or to deal with a proposed development venture. Because of the value and applicability of telemarketing, I have provided the following detailed description for testing this approach and conducting a full-scale fund-raising effort via the phone.

The steps involved in carrying out a telemarketing campaign are:

1. Identify a small, but representative number of prospects to use in a telemarketing test.

Chapter 8 offered suggestions for identifying people who may be affected by your issue. These same people are fund-raising prospects. For the test, randomly select 20 to 50 names from among your prospect list for each volunteer who will participate in the test.

2. List those aspects of the issue that may be of concern to the prospects.

Chapter 2 provided guidance for identifying potential impacts that might result from development and benefits that may be gained if a tract of land is preserved. Both the impacts and the benefits should be presented to prospects during the test to learn which produces the best response rate.

3. Draft a script to use in soliciting support from the prospects. The script must make reference to the concerns identified in step 2.

A telemarketing script has three basic objectives: to find out if the prospect has time to talk, to learn if the prospect is concerned about the issue, and to request support. The following script achieves all three objectives.

"Hello, is this (prospect's name)? Hi, this is your neighbor. . . . I live over on . . . . I'm calling on behalf of the community association. How are you this evening? (WAIT FOR RESPONSE; IF BUSY, THEN SET A TIME TO CALL BACK.) Have you heard about that big highway they want to build through our community? (WAIT FOR RESPONSE; IF NO, THEN DESCRIBE THE ISSUE.) The association met the other night to discuss this situation. We decided that the highway may threaten kids that wander onto the highway, create a real noise problem, cause air pollution in the community, and result in the loss of the nice woodland that's there now. Do any of these problems concern you? (WAIT FOR RESPONSE; NOTE WHICH ITEMS ARE OF CONCERN. IF THE PROSPECT IS NOT CONCERNED AT ALL, POLITELY END THE CONVERSATION.) The association has developed a plan to stop the highway and preserve the quality of life in our community. To carry out the plan, we must raise $5,000. Can we count on you for a contribution? (WAIT FOR RESPONSE.)

The volunteer caller learned if the prospect had time to talk when he asked "How are you this evening?" It is better to pose an indirect question rather then saying, "Do you have time to talk?" People tend to instinctively say no. The caller learned what aspects of the issue caused the greatest concern when he listed the potential impacts and said, "Do any of these problems concern you?" The "ask" came at the end of the script when the volunteer already established that the prospect felt threatened by the issue.

4. Obtain phone numbers for the prospects selected for testing.

If the prospects are members of an organization, ask for a printout of the organization's mailing list along with phone numbers. If you are calling everyone who lives along a given street, check to see if a "criss-cross" directory is available for your area. If you are calling everyone within a given county, town, or election district, check with your local election board. They may provide a listing of registered voters, by street, that includes phone numbers. If all else fails, get your volunteers to look up numbers from the local phone book.

5. Conduct the test.

Spend one evening calling the prospects selected for testing. Calls should be made from 6:00 to 9:00 PM, Monday through Thursday evening. Avoid calling on major holidays and from December 15 to January 5. Keep a careful record of what aspects of the issue were of greatest concern to the prospects. Maintain a record of those who said they were not interested and who pledged support, along with the amount pledged.

So how much did you make during the test? Was it worth the trouble? Will the projected income justify continuing the telemarketing effort? To answer these questions, calculate your overall response rate and the average amount pledged. Now, apply the overall response rate and average pledge amount to the entire list. For instance, let's say the response rate was 40 percent and the average pledge was $20. If you call all 1,000 prospects, you should gain 400 supporters and pledges totaling $8,000. But, usually a maximum of 70 percent of those who pledge will actually mail a check in, if you do everything right. So the actual income would be ($8,000 $\times$ 0.70 =) $5,600.

Finally, to conclude the test, be certain to get a pledge packet in the mail to everyone who agreed to donate during the test. The pledge packet must be mailed as soon as possible, like the morning after the phoning. If you fail to mail out the pledge packet, few of your donors will send you a check. Then everyone will think the test was a failure.

6. Modify the script to incorporate those factors that produced the best results during the test.

Once the test is completed, analyze the results. Were there any impacts that caused particular concern among the prospects? Were there any impacts that few people were concerned about? Revise the script to emphasize the impacts that generated a good response and delete or play down the others. Additionally, the only benefit specifically stated in the script is "to preserve the quality of life in our community." You may wish to substitute more specific benefits if this will improve the response rate.

7. If you noticed any trends in terms of response rate among different "types" of prospects, segment the list so you can call the hottest prospects first.

Did you notice any trends in response rate among prospects with similar characteristics? For example, did the members of one organization pledge at a higher rate than those from another group? Did seniors pledge more then younger people? Was there any relationship between "distance from the site" and the response rate? If you uncovered any trends, segment the list and call the best names first.

8. Locate a facility that has four or more outgoing phone lines and schedule it for one or more evenings of calling.

Businesses are the best place to begin your search for a multiline facility. Ask your supporters if they know of any business that has at least four outgoing lines and preferably 12 to 20. Examples of businesses that may meet these criteria are: real estate offices, law firms, stockbrokers, medical buildings, and insurance offices. Some universities have "telemarketing rooms" that are used in their fund-raising efforts.

If you cannot locate a facility, consider setting up one of your own. The local telephone company can run a number of lines into one location for a short period, say, for a month. They provide the lines, and you provide the phones. Actually, you ask each volunteer to bring along an extension phone from home. The cost to establish a 10-line facility for a one-month period may range from $500 to $1,500. If you keep the phones busy, you can recover the cost many times over.

When all else fails, you can try the creative approach used by one of the author's clients. If you live in an apartment building or in a neighborhood of closely set homes, buy a couple thousand feet of telephone wire, a bunch of modular jack terminals, and run a line from several houses into one. Then have your neighbors bring their phones over for an evening of calling. It worked beautifully for my client.

9. Recruit twice the number of volunteers you need to staff the telephone lines.

Why twice the number? Because usually only half the folks show up. If you get a few extra people, either assign two people to work as a team on one phone or have the poorest callers stuff pledge packets. Start recruiting volunteers well in advance of the first night of calling. Phone each volunteer a day or two before the night of calling to confirm that they will be there.

Once pledges begin to come in,

you can start recruiting your donors to become volunteer callers as well. This allows your pool of active volunteers to expand continually.

10. Prepare a pledge package consisting of a carrier envelope, a pledge form, and a return envelope.

The pledge packet contains materials that remind the donor of how much was pledged and why the donation is so important, and it makes it easy for the donor to send his check in. The pledge packet must be mailed out (first class) the very next day after a pledge is made. If the packet is delayed, the donor will have forgotten the call and your pledge fulfillment rate will decline.

The packet should contain a pledge form that states the amount of the pledge, thanks the donor, describes how to make out the check, and refers to the return envelope. For example:

Dear _____ :

Thank you for your pledge of $____ . Your support is vital to our effort to protect your home and neighborhood from the proposed highway. Please make your check payable to: Community Association, Inc. I have enclosed a self-addressed envelope for your convenience.

Gratefully, _____
(Neighbor who
called you)

The packet should also contain a brief letter or fact sheet describing the issue, your solution, and stressing the importance of the donor's support. The return envelope can be a #6 envelope with the return address imprinted with either a rubber stamp or a label. The envelope containing all these items should be a plain #10. Your return address must be on the outside of the #10 envelope. Use first-class postage, and hand address it if this is practical.

11. Compile phone numbers into a format that will be convenient for your volunteers to use.

If all goes well, your volunteers will be earning your campaign $100 to $150 for each hour they call. Therefore, anything that makes their job easier, keeping them on the phone longer, increases the gross income. Phone numbers should be made available to volunteers in an easy-to-read-and-use format. They should not have to look numbers up. Each minute they spend searching for a number costs you $2.50 per volunteer!

Numbers should be displayed neatly on a page along with the prospect's name and address. Space must be present to note the amount of the donation and any remarks. For example:

Phone
number: 333-3333

Prospect: Jim Jones
            21300 S. Forest Ave.
            Forest, MD 33333

Donation: $50

Remarks: Willing to volunteer

If the prospect does not consent to a donation, a zero is entered under "DONATION AMOUNT". If the prospect agrees to donate but has not decided on a figure, a "?" is entered on the sheet. The "REMARKS" column is used for any information the caller may wish to note.

Each caller will dial about 20 numbers per hour, but will only talk to a dozen people. Sufficient numbers must be available to keep all volunteers well supplied for the entire evening.

12. Mail a letter to each volunteer several days before their first calling session. The letter should discuss the importance of the effort and what will happen during the calling session, and it should help the volunteer to feel at ease. A copy of the script should accompany the letter.

A sample of the letter and a flier entitled "How Does Telephone Fund Raising Work?" is provided at the end of this chapter. Volunteers should be encouraged to rehearse the script before the night of calling.

13. On the night that calls will be made, conduct a half-hour training session, then monitor each volunteer throughout the evening to spot opportunities to offer helpful suggestions.

The training program should review all the items touched on in the letter and flier described in step 12, above. A script covering the entire agenda of a training session is included at the end of this chapter.

Once the volunteers begin calling, visit each. Check the number of pledges they have solicited. If a volunteer is doing poorly, try to find out why. Listen as he goes through the script from a discreet distance. If his presentation sounds okay, try giving him another list of prospects.

14. Promptly mail pledge packets to all those who agreed to donate. This step is self-explanatory.

15. Send thank you notes to everyone who donated time or money. Donors deserve a special thanks for their support. If a thank you note goes out within a month after a donation is made, chances improve considerably that the donor will be a repeat supporter in the future. A simple hand-written note will do just fine.

16. Mail out reminders to all those who have not fulfilled their pledges after four weeks have elapsed since the commitment was made.

Of those who pledge support, usually 70 percent will mail you a check. But it will take at least one reminder to get up to this pledge-fulfillment rate. Usually 35 percent of the donors will send their check within three weeks after receiving the pledge packet. A simple reminder should go out to everyone who has not sent in their donation four weeks after the pledge commitment was made. Some groups send as many as four reminders. How many should you send? Keep them going out until the return is close to the cost of mailing reminders. Following is an example of a pledge reminder:

Dear _____:

On September 7, one of our volunteers called you about our campaign to stop the highway. At that time you pledged a donation of $_____ . Your support is needed now more than ever. Please make your check payable to: Community Association, Inc., and mail it to: 21300 S. Forest Ave., Forest, MD 21200. If you have already mailed your check then please accept our thanks. If you have any questions, call Jim Jones at 333-3333.

Sincerely,

_____

17. Review the results after each night of calling to look for ways to improve the next calling session. Are some callers producing a consistently low response rate? If so, you may wish to assign them to another task. Have any new trends emerged in prospect response rate? Is a different segmentation scheme indicated? If so, you may wish to change the prospect lists assigned to your best callers.

In closing, telemarketing is generally your best source of funding for the organizing and litigation costs associated with a land preservation or development campaign. As you gain experience with a specific fundraising technique, you can begin testing the effects of combining methods. For instance, using direct mail to alert prospects to an upcoming telemarketing or canvassing effort, using telemarketing to sell tickets to an event, or using direct mail to search for people with corporate or foundation contacts. The possibilities are only limited by one's imagination, resources, and time.

LETTER SENT TO VOLUNTEERS BEFORE FIRST EVENING OF CALLING

John Smith
333 Hooper Lane
Forest, MD 33333

Dear John:

Thank you for offering to lend a hand with the Campaign to Save Cromwell Valley on Tuesday, November 29.

In September, a number of volunteers spent an evening calling folks who live near Cromwell Valley. We discovered a surprising level of enthusiasm for preserving the valley. In fact, more than half the people we called pledged their support! We now know that the support is out there to save the valley. The only thing we need to do is ask for it. That's the purpose of the calling we'll be doing on November 29.

On the evening of the 29th, we'll call folks who live near Cromwell Valley. We will alert our neighbors to the impending development that threatens the valley. We will briefly describe our strategy for preserving the valley and offer our neighbors an opportunity to join us in the campaign.

On the evening of Tuesday, November 29, we'll meet at the office of the Clean Water Action Project at 6:00 pm. Their office is located at

2500 N. Forest St., in Baltimore (333-33333).

I have attached a flier describing what will happen at the calling session and a copy of the script we'll be using. You may wish to rehearse the script prior to November 29. Please feel free to bring a friend or two. Give me a call if you have any questions.

Gratefully,

Jim Jones

HOW DOES TELEPHONE FUND RAISING WORK?

The telephone is *the* most effective tool for finding individual supporters for nonprofit organizations. Normally, a group of volunteers meet at a location where a number of telephone lines are available. Following a training session and working from a prepared script, volunteers call people who are likely supporters (prospects) of the organization. The prospects are informed of the importance of the work performed by the organization and the need for support. In a well-managed phone-a-thon, 50 percent of those phoned will pledge support, and each volunteer will net the organization $100 to $150 for each hour they call.

You're Offering a Service, Not Begging!

Your organization does important work. Obviously you support your group because it protects something of value to you. Chances are that you are not alone. There are probably lots of folks who benefit from the services provided by your group. Many of these people might even donate dollars or hours to support your group, if only someone asked.

The purpose of phoning is simply this: to provide those who benefit with a chance to support your group. During the phoning, you'll call, quickly explain you're calling on behalf of your group, ask if the potential supporter is interested, and, if so, explain how he or she can go about pledging support. If the person isn't interested in supporting your group, you'll politely end the conversation.

There's no hard selling involved. Instead, the goal is to get to those folks who are ready to support your organization. In effect, you're offering people a chance to "buy" the service your group provides. By "buying" into your group, new supporters ensure that your good work not only continues, but, hopefully, expands.

The Evening of Phoning

A half-hour training session will begin promptly at the time you were asked to arrive at the phoning location. During the training session, we'll cover the following points: fears we all share about asking for money, how to deal with those fears, why prospects say yes and no, and how to maximize the amount of support for your group.

We'll spend a few minutes reviewing a prepared script. Each of us will read it aloud to another so we can get use to it. You'll be encouraged to modify the script to better fit your own speaking style, but there will be some aspects of the script that must be left intact.

At the end of the first evening, many people find that their worse fears never materialized. More importantly, it was a heart-warming experience to learn that so many people were eager to support the cause.

TELEMARKETING TRAINING SESSION AGENDA

Self-introductions: ask the volunteers to state their names, their role in the group, and why they are here.

Housekeeping: explain where bathrooms are located, the need to keep the facility neat, where refreshments are located, etc.

Explain the purpose of the Phone-A-Thon: describe the issue, the impacts, and your plan to win the issue; describe what the money will be used for; explain that phoning is most effective method of raising funds from individuals and that it also leads to major donors, volunteers, other resources, and builds leaders.

Group Exercises

Go around the room and have each volunteer describe any fears they have. List each fear on a piece of flip-chart paper. Review each fear, and deal with it honestly. Discuss those that are highly unlikely to occur, such as a prospect being rude; those that may happen, such as being asked a question the volunteer can't answer; and, finally, those fears that

will occur, such as prospects saying no. Analyze the reasons why people say no. Make it clear that there are legitimate reasons for saying no. For instance, a prospect may be a realtor and may support the development. The prospect may have a serious illness in the family and cannot afford to donate. Or the issue may simply not affect the prospect.

Explain why fund raising is not begging. See the flier entitled "How Does Telephone Fund Raising Work?"

Discourage volunteers from doing a hard sell. It's a numbers game; volunteers should spend their time getting to the folks who are ready to give.

The Script

Encourage volunteers to modify the script to suit their style, but keep the three basic parts intact.

1. Do you have time to talk?

2. Are you interested in the work our group does?

3. Can we count on you to support our work?

When a pledge is made, have the volunteers verify the spelling of the name, the address, and the amount pledged.

Group Exercise

Have each volunteer turn to the next person and rehearse the script.

Pledge Packet

If volunteer callers will be preparing pledge packets, go over the mechanics of this task.

Conclude the training session by handing out prospect lists and pledge packets, and assign calling stations.

ABOUT THE AUTHOR

Richard Klein has been helping people to deal with land development projects since 1970. He served as the executive director of Maryland's Save Our Streams program for 10 years. He was also a manager with the Maryland Department of Natural Resources for 10 years. During that period, he worked in the water pollution control and fisheries management field. The author is currently the president of Community & Environmental Defense Associates in Maryland Line, Maryland.

ABOUT COMMUNITY & ENVIRONMENTAL DEFENSE ASSOCIATES

Community & Environmental Defense Associates (CEDA) is a consulting firm specializing in helping people to protect their home, community, and environment from the damages associated with land development. CEDA is an association of lawyers, fund raisers, community organizers, scientists, and others who possess the expertise crucial to winning land development issues.

CEDA offers a wide variety of services to support established citizen organizations in their efforts to deal with development. These services include: issue management, the formulation of political action strategy, fund raising, technical analysis of development proposals, the management of land preservation campaigns, power analysis to identify key decision makers, development of legal strategy, legal representation, and a host of other services.

CEDA also supports people in their efforts to win environmental issues, such as landfills, incinerators, well and septic system problems, wetlands destruction, dredging, flooding, stormwater, mud pollution, nuisance conditions associated with lakes and ponds, stream restoration, water quality surveys, mining, sewage sludge disposal, industrial pollution, hazardous waste, and more.

For more information:
Richard D. Klein
Community & Environmental Defense Associates
P.O. Box 206
Maryland Line, MD 21105
301-329-8194